Internet Technology Handbook

Internet Technology Handbook

2002 Supplement

MICHAEL MUCKIAN
AND
RICHARD BARRETT CLEMENTS

PRENTICE HALL

Formerly published as *IS Manager's Guide to Implementing and Managing Internet Technology, 2001 Supplement*

Printed in the United States of America

10   9   8   7   6   5   4   3   2   1

ISBN 0-13-042379-3

ATTENTION: CORPORATIONS AND SCHOOLS

Prentice Hall books are available at quantity discounts with bulk purchase for educational, business, or sales promotional use. For information, please write to: Prentice Hall Direct Special Sales, 240 Frisch Court, Paramus, NJ 07652. Please supply: title of book, ISBN, quantity, how the book will be used, date needed.

PRENTICE HALL
Paramus, NJ 07652

On the World Wide Web at http://www.phdirect.com

How This Supplement Will Help You

The *2002 Supplement* to the *Internet Technology Handbook* (formerly *IS Manager's Guide to Implementing and Managing Internet Technology*) brings you more up-to-date information about many of the fast-developing issues that face IT managers today and offers you guidelines to stay on top of those developments.

You may have heard your colleagues toss around acronyms—XML, ASPs, ISPs, or VOIP; this supplement aims to provide you with an understanding of the latest technologies, as well as help you discern what best fits your needs. In addition, there are discussions of CRM (customer relationship management) technology, Internet branding, and how to negotiate with a technology service vendor.

As the old axiom goes, a carpenter is only as good as his or her tools. The same goes for an information systems professional. Without access to the latest thinking, the most up-to-date software, and the most effective hardware system, you're not going to build anything any time soon. That's true of the largest business and the smaller entrepreneurial firms. In some cases, that's even true for a carpenter.

Nothing changes faster than computer technology and, especially, the online environment. Even the best hardware is outdated and the most current software upgraded by the time you get it installed and operational back at the shop. Keeping up with the competition is more than a matter of market knowledge and business acumen. It's also a function of access to the latest tools and the knowledge to use them. That's where we come in.

Consider this volume your primary tool. It's true that it's only a snapshot in time, but it's probably more current than the snapshot you've been using. And if you pay attention to what you find in these pages, then the value you bring as an IT management professional to your operation will be enhanced, and so will your company's competitive edge.

The *2002 Supplement* offers you insights and ideas about the area that already may be the most critical aspect of your digital operation—the Internet and the World Wide Web. No one quite knows where it's going as an engine of commerce and when—or even if—it will ever get there. But failure to stay current with Internet issues and technology now will cause you serious competitive problems somewhere down the Information Superhighway. Providing you access lanes and on-ramps is the goal of this volume.

As continuing readers know, this is not a stand-alone resource. The *2002 Supplement* is designed to work together with Richard Barrett Clements' excellent *Internet Technology Handbook* (formerly *IS Manager's Guide to Implementing and Managing Internet Technology*). You may have received the two volumes together, or may have received this edition as an ongoing supplement to your original purchase of Clements' 1999 work. Either way, this supplement is not designed to take the place of the original handbook. Rather, this is meant to augment the work with new information about the rapidly changing conditions within the marketplace and IT industry. The two works, taken together, should provide you with all the information you need, at least for this year.

No such work can be created in a vacuum, nor is it prudent not to involve the best resources available to tackle the tougher issues. The same is true of this edition. There are those who know a great deal more than we do about the IT industry. We've tapped the expertise of just a few of those individuals to make sure what we offered you was both current and correct when it came to meeting your information needs.

The following IT professionals constitute the Technology Information Management Team for the *Internet Technology Handbook 2002 Supplement*. We appreciate their contributions and acknowledge the expertise they brought to this book:

- John Bock, Senior Vice President/Chief Information Officer, Community Credit Union, Plano, TX;
- Alan Darbe, Vice President, Information Services, State Employees Credit Union, Lansing, MI;
- Randy Harrington, President, Extreme Arts and Sciences, Inc., Eugene, OR, and
- Connor Sandifer, Director of Information Technology, Boeing Employees Credit Union, Tukwila, WA.

The strong bent toward financial services providers among team members was intentional. As IS heads of their respective retail financial service institutions, team members by necessity are experts on issues as mundane as data processing and as complex as customer relationship management. They're forced to deal with issues relating to financial management, marketing, and retail delivery on a daily basis, as well as maintaining operations for basic business tasks, such as human resources and hardware management. They even deal with the needs of volunteer boards of directors, a factor unique to credit unions. In short, they run all the operations necessary for nearly any business, and then some. And that expertise makes them contributors of the first magnitude.

This volume also could not have been put together without chief researcher Edith Hixson, whose understanding of technology is matched only by her knowledge of where all the good information is hidden. The ability to ferret out the facts puts Edith in a class by herself.

Credit also goes to Prentice Hall editors John Hiatt and Barbara Morris for their contributions, redirection, and streamlining of the text and its purposes. It's a team effort to make this information as relevant to readers as possible. Their strong contributions in this direction will make or break the way the *Internet Technology Handbook 2002 Supplement* helps your business operation. You can thank them for any progress we've made since the *Handbook's* original release.

Most of all, thank yourselves. It's the hard work of those of you in the trenches that has increased the knowledge base in this dynamic new industry that makes such a supplement necessary. True, when it comes to keeping current, you really have little choice. But the desire to compete and succeed in an on-line world is what has driven the growth and progress of both the technology and its applications. That achievement comes from the grassroots level first and involves all of you and the needs of the organizations you serve.

Despite how it may sometimes seem, we can get there from here, thanks to the contributions of individuals like those who contributed directly to this volume, as well as all of you. The *Internet Technology Handbook 2002 Supplement* will, at the very least, point you in the right direction.

Michael Muckian
Madison, Wisconsin

Contents

Chapter S4

CRM Is About the Customer, Not the Technology

23

Chapter S5

Branding Your Internet Identity

35

Chapter S6

The Extra Advantage of Extranets

47

Chapter S7

Not Just Any Portal in the Information Storm

59

Internet Technology Handbook

Chapter S1
Navigating the New Age

To reverse and paraphrase a familiar advertising axiom, this isn't your computer nerd's Internet anymore.

When it comes to information transmission, the Internet has become as ubiquitous in the minds of businesspeople and consumers as the telephone and television. More so, in fact, thanks to the advent and growth of e-mail networks and on-line communities among individuals of all ages, economic and ethnic backgrounds. The fact that you can communicate immediately with anyone anywhere in the world—friend or foe, family or stranger—as part of your local telephone service isn't lost on anyone. For many, it has become the preferred way to share information, especially as the world puts greater and greater demands on our time and the need for a medium that operates and grows among all strata of society.

In the end, we will all become e-mailers, which could change not only the face of business, but our personal lives as well, not to mention the fortunes of the U.S. Postal Service and other commercial carriers. Granted, we'll never be without the need for those friendly men and women in blue who are oblivious to rain, snow, and dark of night. But the fact that the electronic greeting card business and on-line bill payment method are both on the rise should give even the staunchest traditionalist reason for pause. At this rate mail carriers will be delivering only Christmas cards, catalogues and credit card offers, the latter of which also offer on-line service.

Chances are, this growing medium of commerce and chat is not what the creators of the Internet had envisioned back in 1969 when they launched ARPANET, the electronic network that first linked government agencies to researchers. And, as far as business applications go, the idea that this could have become the marketing and sales engine that it already has would have seemed foreign to the point of absurdity. But then again, prior to 1929,

Hollywood moguls never believed that anyone would ever want to hear actors talk. It all goes to show what can happen when technology shows its face at the right place and time.

Knocking on Your Electronic Door

The demand for Internet service is increasing in all sectors and these days, just about everyone is on-line. Statistics from Forrester Research bear this out. According to a recent study, nearly two-thirds of all people under the age of 55 visit on-line sites regularly to accomplish personal and business needs. Usage drops off some after age 55, but not as much as you might think. Nearly 40 percent of those 55 and over use the Internet regularly, and that number is growing.

Moreover, age has little bearing on usage patterns. Whether users are under age 35, between 35 and 54, or over 55, average time spent on the Internet is about 10 hours per week. In fact, those over 55 spend just as much time as those under 35, while the middle group drops off slightly. And the average on-line tenure for each group, or how long they have been wired to the Net, is about three years.

On-line purchase habits are slightly different, with younger users (52 percent) making more on-line purchases than older ones (36 percent), with the middle age group falling squarely in between (49 percent.) But there is great comparability in the use of DSL lines among different user groups (11 to 13 percent), signaling that interest in and use of the Internet for all things will continue escalating as consumers find more routes to faster, easier access.

At these levels of usage, the Internet is not something that businesses can afford to ignore. Whether you believe that on-line commerce represents just another opportunity or will be the medium of choice in future transactions, the numbers are strong enough to support not only the need but the desire for an on-line presence. That goes without saying. How effective you make that presence, on the other hand, will drive how successful you are as well as determine the relative worth of the resources you've allocated to electronic enterprise.

But there are also more insidious forces at work when it comes to the Internet. Numbers are one thing, but quality and purpose of use are quite another. In fact, on-line pundits say, the Internet has reduced the world of commerce to a series of small communities, the members of which may make or break your enterprise in much the same way a customer boycott could have closed the village grocer a century ago.

In the 1970s and '80s physiologists warned us against becoming "couch potatoes," glued to our television screens. These days the greater fear is the proliferation of "computer potatoes," characterized by a PC-addicted population and a social phenomenon fueled by the growth and application of Internet technology. Through its graphic counterpart, the World Wide Web, this powerful medium brings entertainment, information, and especially communication opportunities to anyone with enough money to cover the cost of a modem and the monthly on-line service fees. And increasing numbers of marketers are discovering that their messages can flow through the same pipes, augmenting their other marketing strategies and finding yet another way into consumers' consciousness.

Sounds simple enough, but realize the profound impact the Internet has had on users and the entire marketing equation. Unlike most other remote media—television, radio, print and display advertising—the Internet offers the first truly interactive medium by which marketing messages can be sent and receive an almost immediate response. The couch potatoes may sit back, sip soft drinks and soak up TV spots for the new, improved Whoozit Warfler. The computer potatoes, on the other hand, are accessing the Whoozit Web site, reading design specs, participating in on-line discussion groups, asking questions of the CEO and basically querying the universe as to whether the advertising claims can hold water under close scrutiny.

It's that type of interaction, candid discussion and immediate contact found on the Internet that changes everything. In the book, *The Cluetrain Manifesto,* a variety of authors make the case that the Internet has, indeed, revived the idea of communities. This time, however, it's a not matter of geographic proximity. Communities evolve through an electronic discussion format, which enhances their abilities a hundredfold to literally make or break an idea, an ideology or a marketing or advertising campaign through acceptance or rejection. In 1969, the social cry was "Power to the people!" On-line communications may have finally taken us there.

Slightly Tarnished Golden Opportunities

If you build it, they will come, said the dreamers behind the film *Field of Dreams.* During the '90s, there was an awful lot of building going on in relation to high tech and the Internet. Quite a few people found themselves more than gainfully employed and, in some cases, overnight millionaires when the public discovered that their software doodlings were the answer to one of life's major problems. Toward the end of the '90s, programmers and propellerheads of all stripes and colors called the shots as the industry demanded more and more geniuses to meet the growing demand. For many businesses, cyber life was good.

Such was the case with Sonic Foundry, a Madison, Wisconsin, maker of music and editing software for industrial and entertainment clients. Business for Sonic boomed and the firm experienced a feeding frenzy of hiring. In June 2000, *Madison Magazine*, the local city publication, recognized them as a top contributor to their industry and one of three stellar businesses in this Midwestern community. By December of that year, thanks to a tumble in the marketplace and softening of demand, Sonic laid off 40 percent of its workforce, shaking to the roots the city's fledgling high-tech industry.

The keystrokes on the screen couldn't have been more evident. Despite growing influence and significant spikes in demand and use, high tech suffered the typical ebb and flow any industry experiences as a byproduct of growth. When customer demands increase, companies increase their workforce to keep pace. When that demand slackens, so does the need for those supporting resources. Highly trained tech professionals suddenly found themselves on the street, cast adrift from employers who formerly courted their fancy.

The same holds true with the lost promise of e-commerce. On-line merchants were discovering in increasing numbers that you can lead consumers to cyber opportunities, but you can't make them buy. Security issues, lack of familiarity with the process and a host of other excuses have kept e-commerce at a level of relative infancy, given both its promise and opportunity. Sales through the Internet are increasing, but not at the pace they could be despite discounts and incentives of all kinds. Some dot.com companies have collapsed entirely, while others struggle to keep their heads above water. This, too, has an impact on the high-tech talent floating through cyberspace.

The two situations, though different, make the same point: The proliferation of such talent with no place to go means increased growth just so those who have been displaced through downsizing have gainful employment. In other words, despite the impact of the economic downturn, growth will continue and likely accelerate as this cadre of very talented individuals looks for new ways to use their talent.

Some will resurface as the dot.com industry begins to reinvent itself and reinvigorate the marketplace. Others will undertake new ventures that will, by their very nature, expand the market. Victims of Sonic's fallout, as well as several from Madison-based Guild.com, an on-line seller of art and jewelry that downsized after it was purchased by Houston-based Web retailer Ashford.com, formed 78 Square Design + Technology Cooperative, an entirely new kind of on-line enterprise.

The unique venture, named cheekily after a reference to the firm's host city of Madison as "78 square miles surrounded by reality," offers technology services to smaller clients from a cooperative, employee-owned environment. Their first task, designing a Web site for Planned Parenthood of Wisconsin, shows that even smaller, not-for-profit enterprises can have a home on-line.

Thus, the march to the Web continues, with firms like 78 Square offering less well-heeled clients the opportunity to compete on-line along with the biggest players. And despite earlier trends to the contrary, growth begins again, rising from the ashes of larger initiatives in ways that accommodate the company, the medium and, with any luck, the clients seeking on-line services.

Even the worst conditions can't keep a good industry down. And the conditions faced by technology are far from the worst they could be.

Changing Strategies

As the high-tech industry continues to innovate new ways to accomplish tasks at all levels of sophistication, its role in management—of both the corporate and personal variety—grows in meaning and purpose. Executives who don't have PCs on their desks, laptops in their briefcases and personal assistance devices, such as Palm Pilots, firmly in hand are growing rarer and rarer. Functioning without technology today is much like trying to run a business without telephone service and overnight mail. Frankly put, it can no longer be done.

That technology and the Internet are becoming more and more a part of the management concept is good news. Being competitive in today's business environment requires quick thinking, fast action and immediate access to facts, figures and other data. Only through technology can today's leaders keep up. The bad news is that there is more with which we all have to keep up, and that makes management even more challenging. The purpose of this supplement and the master volume, of course, is to help IS and management executives cope and master the challenges of the new environment.

The best news of all, depending on where you are on the learning curve, is that technology is no longer about transistors, diodes and cathode ray tubes. The concept of high-tech solely as hardware has gone the way of all outdated technologies. Today's concepts revolve around the strategy behind and management of that technology. There are still hardware and software components—what else, after all, defines and identifies technology? But the strategic deployment of those resources by the professionals who run them is the real competitive focal point in this marketplace, and it's one to which even the least technical manager can relate.

There are now distinct steps toward the strategic application and management of technology. It varies from firm to firm and from manager to manager. Good business sense, however, applies as well here as it does in other business settings. If technology can execute operations more effectively and economically, then its application is appropriate. Accomplishing goals through technology, first and foremost, is the foundation of most strategies.

Once that step is mastered, however, there's a higher-level task to undertake. If tasks can be accomplished through technology, then technology becomes a component in the planning process as well as a delivery methodology, making the importance of its intersection with management unmistakable. Using technology to create and facilitate management goals and, more importantly, to manage processes will ratchet up your operation to the levels at which it needs to run to compete. For most businesses anyway, meeting and beating the competition is pretty much what it's all about.

Chapter S2
XML: We're Talking Meta-language Opportunities Here

Comedian Peter Bergman says that, had we all been paying attention, we would have seen Bill Gates coming.

"What is data processing but millions of little gates through which information passes? What does Microsoft do but bill you for passing through all these gates? The name is perfect!"

Data transmission is all about language. If your information can't be understood by the recipient's software, then nothing happens. No data is shared. You don't make your point. The job doesn't get done. End of transmission.

When it comes to the Internet, language becomes even more critical. Millions of transmissions and hundreds of thousands of hyperlink connections every day result in users facing a veritable Tower of Babel when it comes to communication options. Up to now, standard-usage hypertext markup language (HTML) has managed to get most of the messages to most of the people most of the time. Or, in some cases, some of the time. But when it comes to commercial sites that want to do more than act as glorified fax machines, sending and receiving brochureware without interactive capability, the cyber row gets a little tougher to hoe. Suddenly, the World Wide Web, supposedly the real-time lightning rod of communications alternatives, slows to a snail's pace or, worse yet, manages to trip and fall over its own hyperlinks. Either way, data stalls and information is not received.

What's the Problem ?

For all its usefulness, HTML is a limited language, one that operates at a very surface level in order to accommodate the vast amounts of information and a wide variety of systems with which it was originally designed to deal. It was originally meant to operate independently of either user or receiver with an emphasis on simplicity for the user, with portability to take it from one network to the next, and linking capability that allowed users to run strings of data together. In the case of simple two-way, straight-up information transmission, this originally was enough.

And it might still be enough if the supporting infrastructure had been designed to be as complex as its function was to be simple. HTML is a tag language, which means that directions to the system running the language are bracketed at the front and back by instructions that interpret for the receiving system the presentation of that language. Thus, the phrase,

John loves Mary.

would look something like

<A HREF="John.html">John</A>loves<A HREF= "Mary.html">Mary.</A>

which translates into

John loves Mary.

The underlines, of course, are hyperlinks in case the reader wants to know more about either John or Mary. Beyond that, however, we see a lot of unfamiliar tag semantics comprehensible only among computers, limiting just how much information can be and is understood at the receiving end.

Language in the tag semantics—often abbreviated to the point of incomprehensibility—tells us what the operation is about, but doesn't tell what the desired outcome is. We don't learn anything about either John or Mary, which means it lacks whatever intuitive quality might be helpful in furthering the representation of either one on the electronic page received by the reader. In the days of straight data transmission, this might have been acceptable. But as demands for interactivity and, especially, the ability of systems to quickly read the tags in question increase, HTML falls further and further behind.

DRILLDOWN

XML was developed by the World Wide Web Consortium to meet the shortfalls of HTML. It was not designed to make a bad situation worse. As part of its development efforts, W3C crafted what might best be described as the 10 Commandments of XML:

1. XML shall be straightforward to use over the Internet. It shall be as easy to use as HTML, but with all the necessary better features.

2. XML will support numerous applications. It will be grounded in but not limited by its goals of delivering structured documents over the Web.

3. XML shall be compatible with SGML. This is for pragmatic as well as philosophical purposes.

4. Optional XML features shall be kept to a minimum. Since options foster compatibility problems, the ideal number would be 0.

5. XML design should result from quick action, not slow, ponderous IT protocols.

6. Building programs to process XML documents shall be, well, easy. In fact, the easier, the better.

7. XML documents themselves shall be easily created. Simplicity is the key to XML's success.

8. XML documents should be compatible with live-ware (i.e., users and other human beings.) Legibility from a user standpoint is paramount.

9. Terseness and brevity in markup isn't an issue in XML. This is a departure from one of SGML's founding principles, but is designed to make the program more accessible and user-friendly.

10. XML's design shall be formal and concise. This means it should be expressible in EBNF language.

XML Is the Solution

Enter Extensible Markup Language, or XML. As a language, XML maintains the desired simplicity, portability and linking capabilities built into HTML. But it also adds a few other characteristics that put it head and shoulders above its predecessor.

• XML is **intelligent** when it comes to any level of complexity. Want to identify John as that <TALL><DARK AND HANDSOME> at the next desk?

XML can accommodate you. Maybe Mary is the <LOVELY> <BLONDE> woman who works down the hall. XML will note that, too.

- XML is **adaptable** to other environments. It speaks in a common tongue understandable to all other markup languages to the degree of its complexity.

- Above all, XML is **easily maintained.** Its tags include only data and markup. It's look, feel and intuition come from accompanying style sheets, which house the necessary information and keep it from having to be buried in the document notation itself. It's a no muss, no fuss meta-language that doesn't leave nasty residue on the counter, the Web page or anywhere else.

The simple answer to XML's adaptability and appeal is that the tags provide the information itself, not a computer-coded description of the language, and the style sheets do the work of interpreting it. Order something on-line from a catalogue—a blouse, for example—and you'll find a place for the size, the price and the quantity. But in an HTML world, you won't have the option to talk about monogrammed collars or changing the style of buttons from bone to pearl to better match your eyes. Under XML, you can do all that and more.

Both XML and HTML are subsets of Standard Generalized Markup Language (SGML) that drives all systems. HTML was designed and launched because SGML was too cumbersome and costly for all except the largest, most costly exchanges. (Think of HTML as a drone to SGML's queen bee.) SGML is also very general, full of computer-based features designed in an age when every keystroke counted. All in all, it wasn't friendly enough for Joe and Jane Nethead to use on a daily basis.

XML was the answer to what had become a credibility/operability gap. As far back as 1996, members of the World Wide Web Consortium (W3C) were working on a meta-language that combined the best of all worlds, blending complexity with usability to come up with something that would meet the growing sophistication demands of the Web. A meta-language describes and interprets another language, in this case SGML and other Web protocols.

The research team stripped the frills from SGML to create a language that was more streamlined in its approach and more digestible to the common user. XML was first launched in 1998 and has been growing in popularity and use ever since. Virtually anyone with a modicum of computer sophistication can master the rules of XML, creating files from scratch that can be read by any markup language system, as well as any user able to access such a system. In addition, the program was structured such that any single system, often called a parser, would be able to process the language. In short, thanks to the buried style sheets, XML is more robust, more user-friendly and more adaptable to complex tasks.

XML presents a unified approach to the challenges it faces, thanks to a few simple and well-used characteristics of its design, first and foremost of which is its nesting structure.

Like HTML, XML uses descriptive tags, which almost always come in pairs, creating a structure known as a "tree." Within the tree, as within a genealogical tree, there is a relationship among the elements depending on how the information is presented within that tree. There is no question, no ambiguity about how these elements relate to each other. This makes it easier for users, especially programmers, to position and display the information and for systems to interpret the data.

XML also relies on Unicode, a character-encoding system that supports the intermingling of all the world's major languages. Software able to read English, for example, probably doesn't recognize characters from Japanese. XML deals with any combination of character sets, which enables communication not only between different computer systems, but also between different countries, ethnic groups and languages. The only thing XML doesn't do is transport data from one application to another. That honor belongs to Enterprise Application Integration, better known as EAI.

DRILLDOWN

XML speaks the language, but EAI makes sure it's delivered to all who can read it. Enterprise Application Integration (EAI) creates a direct link between applications that promotes data transmission in real time. This is different from earlier manifestations, including electronic data interchanges (EDI) and other methodologies that did periodic data dumps between systems to which they were connected. Today's EAI is more flexible and serviceable thanks to upgrades by major high-tech companies and revised standards brought about by the rise in popularity of XML, including EAI vocabularies more specific to business needs.

Revolutionizing the Web

Thanks to excessive traffic and regressive HTML capabilities, critics have begun to refer to the World Wide Web as the World Wide Wait. As XML spreads, reducing wait time may initially be the most evident, but ultimately will be the least valuable of its contributions. The structure and ease with which XML will enable users to communicate and create commerce on-line will profoundly affect the way we all approach the Net. Its impact simply can't be overestimated.

Consider on-line discount travel programs, for example. XML capabilities, matched with those of Java scripts imported from the host computers, can make complete functionality and capability as close as your palmtop device and infinitely more responsive. Request a download of all flights from New York to Paris and you likely will receive a list as long as your arm and much longer than your screen shot allows. Before you decide, you're going to have to sort. If that list is delivered with a small Java program that allows the sort to take place on your desktop, laptop or palmtop—rather than back at the travel agency's server terminal with a thousand other similar requests—then you take tremendous pressure off the host computer and accomplish your goals in a fraction of the time. HTML could never support this effort; XML can.

Your trip through cyberspace on hyperlinks will also be improved with the advent of Xlinks, a more sophisticated version of the technology. In addition to allowing direction to multiple destinations, Xlinks will connect directly to the appropriate point in the database, rather than simply going from page to page. This will eliminate the frequency of broken hyperlinks (the "404 File Not Found" error message could become a thing of the past) as well as define new ways of researching on the Web. Creation of a Resource Description Framework (RDF) system has been a parallel project to XML creation. RDF is designed to develop meta-data that will make Web searches faster, easier and more accurate. After XML, that will be the next great growth engine on the Web.

DRILLDOWN

XML also has the capability to render data and information in Braille or even as audible speech. Quite obviously, this is a huge advantage for the visually impaired and, in the case of audio, for anyone who needs to access information while behind the wheel of a car.

The Impact on e-commerce

The strength, simplicity and facility of XML and its related technologies will help revolutionize the way companies do business on the Web, both from a resource and an access standpoint. The dot.com falloff of 2000 may find itself to be a phoenix rising from the ashes, with new engines of opportunity at its disposal. But you had better be ready to meet the challenge if you don't want this phoenix to turn into a turkey before your very eyes.

The transition to an XML format is critical for firms that want to do more than mere e-marketing. Sending the sales message is critical, but being able to present options and execute the order in ways that serve rather than frustrate customers is the way to close sales instead of chasing Web surfers away. The fact that XML is based on SGML protocols which, in turn, are based on ISO standards, indicates uniformity within industry and the likelihood that it will be an evolutionary technology, the foundations of which will be around for some time.

XML's complexity will lead to true connectivity between buyer and seller, wholesaler and retailer. Your inventory linked directly to your supplier's warehouse through a live, real-time uplink means that merchandise will be automatically shipped when supplies run low. That not only keeps the shelves stocked but supports all the economies of just-in-time inventory that we've learned over the last decade.

We've already discussed to a degree the way attached Java files can help reduce user dependence on the host computer. The impact on a company's IS resources could be profound, freeing them up to perform other, more developmental tasks or reducing the amount of necessary memory space. Perhaps this is simply the next generation of the self-service gas station and other strategies designed to off-load more of the service work on consumers, or perhaps this is something completely different. Either way, its financial and operational impact shouldn't be underestimated.

Speaking of extensions, when you get right down to it, XML will be the heart of e-commerce in the future. Throughout history, business has been built around uniform documents—invoices, bills of lading, receipts and other standardized documents—that described the necessary components of the transaction in progress without excess information and in a form both the buyer and seller could understand.

When HTML was written, it was to provide access to general information, not to promote commerce. XML, on the other hand, was born for this. The big difference is that, rather than simply providing uniform documents, the program also offers complex interactive processes that facilitate the entire business process. When it comes to e-commerce, there's no better engine than XML.

Beyond e-commerce

There will be life after the current generation of XML, but it will be at the hands of intelligent Web agents and other sources that not only facilitate the data as per user instructions, but actually anticipate and fill the need before they are asked to do so. Mathew Fuchs of Disney Imagineering says it this way: "Information needs to know about itself, and information needs to know about me." And that speaks to a more intuitive, intelligent Web and the programs that power it.

Consider a personal shopping agent, a bot with a penchant for your preferences. It's like a variation on Amazon.com purchase recommendations, but one that combs the Web in search of your favorite scent, flavor, or color, providing a wealth of opportunities to you before you even ask.

Perhaps you encode your credit card number and empower it to purchase certain items in specific colors and within predefined price limits. In unusual situations, you may even allow it to exercise its own judgment and make purchases of rare items available in limited quantities or favorite brands available at a deep discount. ("It was a closeout sale on case lots of Chateau Margaux at a price I just knew you wouldn't want me to pass up, Sir.")

Of course, this would require an extremely sophisticated, "intelligent" Web agent. As for the system driving the selection process...well, XML is already here.

Chapter S3
From Aggravation to Aggregation

As we said in the previous chapter, data transmission is all about language. If your information can't be understood by the recipient's software, then nothing happens.

Music, at least of the vocal variety, is all about language, too. As in the case of opera, you may not always understand the words, but if you can't appreciate the musical "language," then true communication—translated as "appreciation"—can't take place.

In the case of music, it's also the ability of the vocalist that determines the quality of the communication. Plainly put, if he or she ain't got the pipes, then whatever comes out may not be worth appreciating. The same holds true in Internet data transmission: If the pipes can't carry sufficient amounts of data with the speed and integrity for which they were designed, then they won't be singing your song for very long.

The data traffic jam has reached crisis proportions, especially on the average users' side, as more and more transmissions require greater and greater amounts of bandwidth in which to travel. A small video editing shop we know has stopped sending rough-cut videotapes to commercial clients in favor of e-mailing snippets that can be video streamed into the clients' computers to allow them to give the necessary approval before the editors move forward into final production. Does video streaming save the client time and money? You bet it does. Does it make the video editing shop seem more professional and in touch with the technology of the 21st century? It is definitely one of the coolest ways to do business today.

Does the transmission add to the Internet Info Jam? Even the chief editor admits that it's sometimes like trying to cut through cross-town traffic at

15

rush hour, even when your info superhighway travels along the DSL Line. Too much of a good thing makes even the Internet a dull medium.

This is where aggregation comes in. In the same way we periodically need to clean our hard drives to make sure holes and spaces haven't developed among the data, wasting precious disk space and causing bumps and bruises to our files as the computer attempts to scan smoothly across potholes in the information, file aggregation prior to transmission can help make the system run more smoothly. Sometimes it comes down to aggregating the lines themselves, other times creating displays at the user end that combine like information from different portions of the database for ease of use. In either situation, data integrity and ease and speed of transmission improve, facilitating better results from the technology at hand.

Aggregation Defined and Implemented

The term *aggregation* refers to a number of alternative solutions to issues facing the on-line world and we will handle each of them in turn. For the sake of clarity, however, let's define the concept of aggregation in the abstract with an eye toward better understanding its concrete applications.

Scientifically speaking, aggregation is a model that displays an object class made up of one or more component object classes. For example, the basement and first floor are subcomponents and part of the aggregate known as a building. The aggregate may not exist without its subparts, but the nature of the aggregate relationship applies participation constraints to each of the subparts involved in the aggregate. The second floor of that building, in point of fact, would not be a second floor without the structure, goals and restrictions of the building itself. If that second floor existed at all, it would exist simply as another "floor" somewhere in time and, especially, in space. Without the benefit of the structure and constraint defined by the aggregate, the identity and application of the subcomponents would be irrelevant.

Simplistically speaking, your average zoo is an aggregation of sub-object classes such as lions and tigers and bears (oh my!), not to mention seals and monkeys and elephants, among other creatures. The zoo becomes the aggregate of these subcomponents and would not be a zoo without these subcomponents. Without the aggregate of the zoo, the lions, tigers and bears would not change their identities, but they would not have the added characteristic of being zoo residents.

The same goes for a martini, which is an aggregate of the subcomponents gin (a distilled beverage), vermouth (a fermented beverage) and an olive and/or lemon twist (for some a daily serving of vegetables and/or fruit). Without the benefits of its subcomponents, it would not be a martini. Without the structure of the martini, the singular components would be no more than they are.

On-line aggregation is a little less colorful, but no less critical. It's basically a strategy that takes independent transmission resources and joins them to create a whole technology greater than the sum of its individual parts. This on-line gestalt is designed to provide swifter, more effective access to the Internet in the face of increasing technological and informational demands.

At the receiving end, the concept of aggregation turns around and transforms itself from a transmission strategy to a recipient methodology. In other words, information categorized digitally in a variety of ways and from a variety of sources can be grouped and categorized for easier, more logical digestion. Right now, the financial services industry is struggling with this challenge in account presentment to customers. We'll talk about this at some length later in this chapter.

Whether we're theoretical or concrete, effective aggregation means that no matter what kind of gridlock you face when trying to enter the information superhighway, with a little effort you can get there from here if you know which on-ramps to access.

DRILLDOWN

High-speed Internet access has become a competitive strategy for multiple-tenant units (MTUs), such as apartments and condominiums under constructions, as well as hotels, airports and wherever particular Netheads congregate. The purpose, of course, is to provide services to residents and travelers that help them solve the bandwidth dilemma. A Cahners' study predicts this trend will increases the sale of MTU broadband equipment and services from $370 million in 2000 to $4.8 billion in 2004.

Strike Up the Broadband

What it comes right down to is a matter of bandwidth. In other words, the amount and speed of information your computer can transmit over the

Internet tends to depend on the capacity of the line or lines that you are using. In other words, how fast your pipe is will control the success or failure of your transmission behavior. In the same vein, the lack thereof will effectively restrict success, further determining your level of need for greater aggregation of access and retrieval resources.

In many cases, there may be no need at all. The small video editing shop to which we referred earlier solved a lot of its problems with the installation of a digital subscriber line (DSL) designed exclusively for transmission of digital information. The average phone line still works, but it's slower and less reliable. A DSL line presents a thicker "pipe" and works much better, but is much more expensive to operate and maintain. For the home user, there's always the option to install a second phone line; for commercial accounts interested in single-line access, DSL is the only option. Chances are, in most cases, a DSL line could also negate the need for aggregation, at least from the transmission side.

The big complaint about DSL, in addition to the fact that it can cost three to five times as much as a standard phone line, is that it's not available in all markets. That's changing rapidly, which means that the number of travelers on this high-intensity line has increased dramatically.

According to a survey conducted by TeleChoice, a telecommunications industry consulting firm, there were slightly fewer than 3 million DSL lines in operation at the end of first-quarter 2001. With a record of an average 15 percent increase per quarter throughout the previous year, this means an estimated 4.5 million DSL subscribers entering 2002 with no end to growth in sight. Continued demand for accurate access, plus computer files growing in size and complexity mean that, despite the cost, demand for DSL access will continue to meet the supply of lines and market available.

For those users who can't or won't invest in DSL, cable modem or other broadband technologies, aggregation still remains an option. Multiple lines gathered and run as high-performance clusters (HPCs) offer very economical options for a large variety of parallel and distributed networks. In addition, they can be surprisingly effective in carrying significant data to and through the Internet, operating in some cases even more effectively than DSLs.

Understanding how this concept works can help you decide whether or not this is something that can and should work for you. Before we talk about the components of aggregation, however, consider the following benefits of the average aggregated system, particularly as it operates as an information retrieval tool:

- Well-deployed aggregate resources can simultaneously query numerous sources, creating a single access point to the most relevant Internet information, increasing access speed, improving results and enhancing overall productivity. Since these results appear in real time and most systems keep a record of searches made, information updates can be rapidly and accurately done.

- Most aggregation systems include an installation program and rely on a simple Web-based administration tool that can customize searches to the parameters designed by the users and their departmental or organizational needs. Once again, productivity is enhanced and the value of retrieved information is increased through customization.

- In order to be effective, an aggregation program must be compatible with standard operating systems. As such, the program makes ease of use and the relative "invisibility" of the aggregator itself paramount, which means more access, and distribution and retrieval with fewer errors and broken connections.

Companies that pursue aggregation should first understand what the options are before striking out on a path. There are some key considerations when it comes to building bandwidth that are a part of any good aggregation scenario.

DRILLDOWN

Part of any aggregation scenario is the concept of bonding, an exercise that occurs when a Web server segments information—a picture file, for example— into several data packets for easier transmission over an aggregate line. Rather than trying to digest one larger file, the data packets provide several files that most systems find easier to handle. Codes are sent along with the data packets that essentially describe the segmentation along with instructions for reconstruction. The data packets are delivered to the Web server at the other end, which reassembles the packets into the same image or file that it was prior to transmission.

A Simple Concept

When it comes right down to it, aggregation is a cost-effective way to increase bandwidth—the size of the pipes leading from your computer to the Internet and back—to improve performance and increase capabilities to send and receive complex files. Internet access bandwidth—the connection between your computer and the Internet—often is the weakest link in the information chain. Aggregation can enhance access capabilities and improve your connection.

In many cases, it can also be cheaper than the standard 256K DSL line. Three 56K modems operating in tandem don't quite replicate the full capacity of one DSL line, but they come close to doing the job for most operations. And that may be enough for your needs.

There are two basic types of scenarios to consider as you approach aggregation:

- There is an extension of standard point-to-point protocol (PPP) called **PPP Multilink Protocol** (MP) that aggregates transmission by bonding two simultaneous parallel connections. The end result is a virtual connection, the bandwidth of which is equal to the sum of the two parallel links. Information transmitted over the lines may be fragmented into packets (see sidebar on page 19) to meet maximum transit unit values, or sent as whole files depending on the bandwidth space available. As described above, the messages are divided and sent over the two parallel lines and must be recombined at the receiving end.

  PPP Multilink is a public standard and subject to greater interoperability among vendors. When the technologies are identical at either end, then downloading will be twice as fast because no translation need take place. The relative transparency between users assures a more seamless edit of both data and process than on other systems. If there is any drawback, it's that both the sender and receiver must be operating with the same pair of endpoints. Not all connection types are supported by PPP Multilink, which means you need to know before sending just what type of hardware and software will be receiving your message and what kind of support you can expect.

- There is also a protocol called **connection teaming** which operates much the same way as a phone center distribution system works.

Different computer modems are connected through a local area network (LAN for short) and transmission through the Internet is sent out on whatever available line can carry the traffic. That way there is little or no waiting for linking availability. The user rarely knows which line he or she is transmitting on, but that doesn't really matter.

Unfortunately, connection teaming does not segment data, so large files take as long to send as they would on a straight modem line. The advantage comes in the case of multiple users needing ongoing access to the Internet. That's when connection teaming's distribution strategy is most valuable.

There is even a case that can be made for connection teaming's use by a single Internet user. Realize that most Web sites consist of dozens of graphic characters, many of which have their own http protocol. Connection teaming treats each of these elements in the same way it does LAN connections, brining the components back on several lines simultaneously. This makes for a quicker, more efficient connection for the user.

Which to choose? If you have a choice and you don't require mix-and-match capabilities among a variety of modems or have multiple users on a LAN—connection teaming's two special skill sets—then PPP Multilink would be the protocol of choice. It creates a transparent, seamless transmission that breaks data down into packets when necessary. Analog modem or ISDN line users will realize superior results from PPP Multilink. Plus, it's available from most Internet service providers.

The Coin's Other Side

Just to leave no computer node unturned, it's important that we mention the other side of aggregation. That concerns the blending of files on-screen for e-commerce purposes, the better for customers to see what related products and services might be offered by a retailer, even if these products originate from different files and, indeed, different databases.

The financial services industry is struggling with this right now in its attempts to put all customer account information into one screen shot, so that customers can check their savings balances, investments, loans and other financial activities without having to jump screens and do their own calculations to determine their financial net worth. Since each of these activities likely generates from a different database, executing what seems like a relatively easy concept can be a challenge. But according to a survey by the Gartner Group, a financial industry think tank, customers are willing to pay extra for such a service, which means banks will have to offer such information in order to stay competitive.

Wells Fargo & Co. and J. P. Morgan Chase & Co. already have such processes in place. And Citibank's site is available to anyone who has an account anywhere in the U.S. Screen-scraping technology and access to aggregate data from 1,500 banks and other sources nationwide make this possible. It's clear that, when it comes to aggregating sites and services to stay competitive in the marketplace, today's e-retailers have only just begun.

Chapter S4

CRM Is About the Customer, Not the Technology

Management theories come and go, but the customers spring eternal. Without the customer, there would be little reason and no opportunity for you to be in business. The customer may not always be right, but he or she is the one in position to make the purchase that provides the revenue to fund your business enterprise and, by extension, your flashy new BMW or your kids' orthodontia. When customers talk, you need to listen; otherwise, they may start talking to your competition.

For our purposes, this all boils down to the acronym CRM, which stands for customer relationship management. Or, if you prefer, e-CRM—electronic customer relationship management. In either case, the word "customer" is the dominant element. When it's used at all, the *e* that stands for "electronic" is cast in lowercase, just as it often is in "e-commerce." This is by design, not accident, and is used to stress the main point: CRM is about the customer, not about the software used to support said customer's purchase activity. Technology exists to serve customers. Customers do not exist to give technology something to do.

That may be a difficult concept for some technocrats to grasp and woe to the organization that fails to understand and apply that guiding principle. Your customers come to you because they can get the product or service they want or need in a fashion that suits their lifestyle and at a price that fits their budget. Your customers don't care what kind of software you use to manage these tasks on their behalf. They only care about having their needs met. Never forget that.

Your Strength Is Your Weakness

Ironically, the very aspect that enables you to better serve customers—whether that be through on-line shopping opportunities, e-mail network development or customer service (call) centers—is also your Achilles' heel. The very technology upon which you've come to rely has enabled a wider array of competitors to get into your game. Companies that heretofore might have existed merely as local or perhaps regional outlets can now go global with the help of a Web site, something that can be set up in a relatively short time. You may be the industry leader with 100 years of experience. But now that the newest kid on the block can tap into the same toolbox you're using, you begin to look painfully like all the rest of them. It's CRM that helps separate the leaders from the followers.

Wait, the equation becomes even more challenging. In addition to dealing with an increasing number of Web-savvy competitors, you'll have to satisfy customers who have become more critical of your efforts and more nimble in pursuit of other options. Dissatisfied consumers no longer are willing to go gently into that good night. Thanks to Web chat rooms and e-mail, they tell each other frequently and with alarming candidness—and that extends to friends as well as complete strangers—just how horrible your services are and even challenge you directly as to why you've failed to meet their expectations and beat the competition. The customer has become an even more potent force than in the past, which puts extra pressure on you to provide excellent customer service or suffer the consequences.

This chapter isn't about the latest and greatest customer management software. It isn't about system configuration to better enable improved customer service performance. It doesn't concern itself with technical tips, tricks and techniques to help you gain the competitive edge. Chances are you already know most of that and that what you don't know will change and improve even before you finish reading this chapter. What we're going to talk about is the need for an effective corporate philosophy that meaningfully supports CRM, as well as ways that technology can help support those corporate goals.

Chances are if you know *why* your firm is vigorously pursuing CRM—and if it's not you may want to find yourself another firm—you will be better able to determine *how* you can most effectively support that effort. You will also understand that providing support through more fully automated systems and a variety of response mechanisms will be critical to continued success.

The High Price of Customer Acquisition

New technologies have increased the speed and improved the quality with which we serve our customers. That's a fact, Jack. But the cost of acquiring and keeping new customers was, is and always will be higher than the cost of serving current customers. Studies time and again have shown that that's a fact, too, Jack. Consider, for example, the following relatively recent revelations by some leading experts in the field:

- According to a study by the Boston Consulting Group, it costs $6.80 to market to existing customers on the Web, while marketing to new customers weighs in at $34 a head.
- According to *Industry Standard*, a now-defunct trade publication, it costs on-line companies an average of $250 to acquire a new customer. That customer spends lightly—$24.50 during the first quarter after acquisition—in the beginning, but then averages $52.50 per quarter after the first one for the life of the relationship.
- Despite that seeming good news, roughly 65 percent of all Web customers never make a second on-line purchase.

In effect, all that new Shiva the Destroyer software you've installed to chart purchase progress, price sensitivity and a host of other customer data won't do much good if your strategies for hanging on to the 35 percent that bring repeat business to your Web site aren't sound. That's the function of CRM and it's an investment well worth its price. Statistics, once again, bear this out:

- A study by Accenture (formerly Anderson Consulting) notes that the typical billion-dollar high-tech firm can add up to $130 million in profits by effectively managing customers. In fact, researchers said, as much as 64 percent of the return on sales between average- and high-value customers is the result of good CRM practices.

- According to McKinsey & Co., a 10 percent increase in repeat business often adds up to a 10 percent increase in bottom-line figures. That contrasts to the value of a 10 percent savings on marketing and advertising costs, the yield on which is a measly 0.7 percent.

What those numbers tell us is that CRM is a proactive, not a reactive strategy designed to increase participation rather than decrease defection. You can rig all the Web traps you want to make it harder for customers to exit your Web site without making a purchase. That's the old "make it easy for 'em to buy" strategy from direct mail taken to a higher and more hyper-active level. That's also the difference between a prison cell and a garden party. You don't want customers to hang around just because they can't get out. All that will mean is that, once they do exit, they will never come back. And whether you're high-tech or low, the old adage that repeat customers pay the bills still applies.

What Is CRM?

Understanding the concept behind the catchphrase is the first step in getting the right system in place to meet your company's needs. There are different views and variations on the definition, but according to the CRMGuru.com Web site, the official definition is as follows:

> Customer Relationship Management is a business strategy to select and manage customers to optimize long-term value. CRM requires a customer-centric business philosophy and culture to support effective marketing, sales and service processes. CRM applications can enable effective customer relationship management, provided that an enterprise has the right leadership, strategy and culture.

Please note that nothing is said about "the right software" or "the proper platform configuration." For too many firms, CRM is driven by the best software package that money can buy. Good tools are critical and no CRM system can be executed today without complex software configurations necessary to balance all the elements. But firms that think CRM is only about what their computer system can do and not grounded in sound management philosophy and zealous company commitment are doomed to fail. And to fail expensively.

In fact, CRM hinges on actively deepening your knowledge about current and potential customers and, if need be, reengineering operational systems to capitalize on that knowledge and serve those customers. CRM is not a technical solution; however, technology plays a big part in CRM applications. The more important facet is the belief and commitment by the company to make effective CRM happen.

That's not to say, however, that CRM applications don't mean big business for software companies. In fact, AMR Research estimated that at its current growth rate of 50 percent per year, the market for CRM applications would hit $5.4 billion in 2000 and continue to climb. Other studies boast even higher figures, with the Aberdeen Group's estimated annual sales of hardware, software, peripherals and related licensing agreements totaling $7.8 billion in 1999, of which $3.8 billion was for software alone. By 2002, that market is estimated to climb to $10 billion annually.

With those types of dollars at stake, it's easy to see why CRM pops up in many minds as a software application first and a management philosophy second. It's not easy to let go of those funds in favor of philosophy, but companies that don't have that solid underpinning will be making a costly strategic and operational error.

DRILLDOWN

Know your customer as you would yourself and you shall be prosperous. That's true to a point, but you also have to know the nature of your product, its transaction modalities and external forces affecting the sale if you're going to be successful. Customer loyalty in the financial services industry is valuable to a point, and that point is usually the interest rate on big-ticket items such as car loans or mortgages. The best CRM program will do you little good if your mortgages, for example, are priced a full point above market or your car loan rates can't meet or beat the competition. In this case, price more than service is the deciding factor. Understand that before entering into the game and your CRM efforts will have a better chance of staying on track.

Who Are Our Customers?

In the old days, customers had unfailing loyalty, first to the town merchant, then to his or her favorite brands. Despite the seeming dichotomy between the two, the reasons were the same: a) the customer often had no other real options to turn to; and b) the customer, through trial and error, built up trust in either the merchant, the brand or both. From that trust, loyalty emerged because the merchant and/or brand proved reliable and consistent.

Generating loyalty today, especially with on-line purchases, is much the same type of exercise. Of course, there are dozens and sometimes hundreds of choices, which makes reliability and consistency paramount. These are the core elements of CRM. Today, however, there's a need for more than merely great service expertly delivered. Managing relationships with customers means understanding those customers, getting inside their heads and hearts and knowing what their preferences in your product are as well as they know them themselves. That takes a lot of time and effort and can run to high levels of expense. And that means who the customer is and how valuable his or her level of business will be just got more important.

Effective CRM is about generating share-of-wallet relationships with customers. The more goods and services they buy and the more frequently they buy them are the units of measure for that wallet-share value. Your software needs to be able to track, analyze and report that information so that decisions can be made as to how much time, effort and expense you're willing to invest in this person. And one of the secrets to knowing your company's ability to serve its customers, first and foremost, comes from knowing yourself. Who do you want to be? What market niche do you want to serve? How does all this tie in with your business plans? Know that and you're on your way to forging effective customer relationships.

What it boils down to, first and foremost, is a question of value. It's the value you bring to the customer, balanced by the economic value they add to your firm that can make CRM a hit-or-miss proposition. Are you pursuing customers that don't fit your average repeat-client profile? If so, you may be wasting time and effort attempting to cultivate a market segment that doesn't exist. Moreover, if you're attempting to position yourself as the most innovative firm in the industry when, in reality, the buying public views you as "the old reliable," you again may be wasting time, money and effort. Know your customers, then know yourself and look for the levels at which the two intersect most profitably. That's where your competitive advantage lies and that's the level at which you will want your system to interact.

Design a product, service and delivery mechanism that is consistent from product to product, sale to sale, customer to customer. Too many of us wrestle with problems within our own computer systems, making it difficult enough to visit your Web site and make purchases. We don't have the time and energy to help you adjust to your own growing pains. Good customer relationships start with ease of access. (Make it easy for 'em to buy, remember?) The cornerstone of that ease is knowing what to expect and having as little deviation as possible in process and procedures. Life is challenging enough. The less challenging you make this part of it for us, the more we like you.

Finally, make sure the operation of your system is as low-cost as possible. One of the foundation principles of working with technology is reduction in cost and automation of operations. Work hard to preserve that. As more competition enters the market, your margins are squeezed even tighter, making turning a profit a tenuous thing. You and others have worked hard to get customers attuned to doing business on the Net. Now that you have them trained, make sure you're able to follow through fully. Otherwise, the next generation will figure out ways to eat the lunch you've worked so hard at cultivating and growing.

Remember, your goal is to make customers loyal on-line purchasers. Evolving a system that works because of experience—both yours and theirs— is the best way to develop and cultivate your CRM strategy. That's partly technology, partly philosophy and a lot of good customer service rolled into an airtight operating structure. No more, no less.

Implementing Your CRM Efforts

We've spent a lot of time talking about developing corporatewide CRM philosophies and have touched little on how systems can be implemented in your company. Well, guess what? We're going to talk about that philosophy a little more as part of implementation because undoubtedly there are still people who think they can cut right through all this soft stuff and move on to hard-core systems purchases. That's a little like buying a car before you learn how to drive or ordering clothes from a catalog without knowing your size.

You need to understand the prep work as part of the process before moving forward.

First and foremost, your system will have to be customer-centric in order to succeed. That means it will have to conform to the needs of the customer first, then the company second. That means listening to the customer and sharing information that will aid him or her in making a purchasing decision. Please note: Marketing "spam" doesn't count in the on-line scenarios of today. Remember that you're managing a relationship, not selling a used car. Your customers may never be your friends, but they will need to feel friendly toward your Web site and the way you do business if you want them to make purchases.

Even though that sounds simple, it will result in highly complex systems that combine a variety of media for maximum effect. Your Web site must effectively display and describe your products and services if you want to interest customers. (That's one technology.) But there will also need to be a response mechanism so those with unusual questions can e-mail you for more information. (That's a second technology.) Of course, your e-mail system will be automated for ease of operation, but you will also need consumer-friendly liveware—that would be an attendant available to answer questions—to handle incoming e-mails that require personal attention. (That's at least a split in the second technology, if not the addition of a third.)

Many companies forget that customer service centers—formerly known as "call centers"—are also part of this equation, and that's an entirely different ballgame. Nevertheless, technology supporting those centers must be linked to on-line systems so operators have access to all previous transaction information. The worst thing that can happen to a customer relationship is forcing customers to tell their stories more than once, especially during the same call. They're going to get frustrated, hang up and never call back. And that's precisely what you don't want to happen.

Finally, there's fulfillment and that's where the rubber does or doesn't meet the road in terms of service. Orders incorrectly shipped and sent do more to damage a company's CRM profile than just about anything else. This means there need to be direct links between the Web site, the call center and the warehouse. Fulfillment is the climax to any customer relationship; all the rest is foreplay. Unless you want to be known for your commercius interruptus, you'll need to make sure the technology is seamless from the time the customer picks up his or her telephone to the time the delivery service drops the package off at his or her door. Then you can sit back and have that cigarette.

Redefining your approach, however, is only the first part of your strategy. The next step is to look at what you do to see how customer centricism does or doesn't mesh with your basic operational strategy. It shouldn't be a revelation to anyone that when you change your business philosophy, you must change the way in which you do business, sometimes dramatically so. And if you don't change that approach, then nothing substantial will happen.

This is often one of the most difficult concepts for a company to accept because it is often one of the most difficult tasks to perform. In a lot of cases, one of two things can happen:

- The management team and key staff talk about changing to a customer-centric philosophy, examine the reasons and methodologies to do so and agree that this is the right and proper thing to do. They might even hug. But then the plan is never executed and nothing gets done, ergo nothing changes.
- The management team and key staff talk about changing to a customer-centric philosophy, then instruct IT to go and find the proper software to make it happen. IT spends a bunch of money, takes a lot of time and in the end creates a system that no one can use and that doesn't work like it's supposed to. In that case, management either blames IT for the company's failure to move to CRM or agrees that it won't happen until the next software upgrade.

Of course, this is the stuff of which "Dilbert" cartoons are made. The key issue here is that whenever a company tries to move from being operations-centric or stockholder-centric or whatever-centric it is to being customer-centric, it has to change the way it does things. The company has to work differently, otherwise it will keep getting the same results. And new results, presumably, are why the company is changing its approach in the first place. This may come down to reconfiguring the organization, redeploying employees to new tasks, stopping some old activities, starting some new ones, and otherwise reinventing itself. What's more, it may have to be done in consort with customer input, and we all know what that means in terms of operational challenges. But it's a matter of paying the piper now or later. Be prepared to bite down hard and do whatever it takes to make the necessary adjustment, or things are not going to change. Not really. Remember the old saying: If you continue to do what you've always done, you'll continue to get the results you've always gotten. Like a lot of old sayings, this one works every time.

Redesigning your functional activities runs part and parcel with reengineering work processes. This should go without saying. You can talk about CRM, embrace it conceptually and buy software to support it. But if you don't change functional operations and reengineer processes to accommodate your company's evolution to CRM, then your efforts won't be successful. Often, this involves merely changing the order in which we do things, which may or may not be successful. Unlike straight operations, however, CRM relies heavily on the input and influence of the customer, both of which are notoriously unreliable. Concentration on making the process as smooth and uninterrupted as possible from the time the first marketing contact is made until the product is delivered might be a better, more effective strategy.

DRILLDOWN

There are right ways and wrong ways to handle CRM management and implementation. Consider the following implementation strategies:

- Assign project managers who have addressed CRM issues before. The implementation process will go smoothly and it won't be a case of the blind leading the blind.

- Design business events from the customer interaction viewpoint by tracing associated processes through the enterprise and analyzing movement of data, handling consistency and feedback.

- Make sure your strategy is built on small- to medium-sized steps that migrate to sound business, technology and implementation solutions.

Time for Software

Once the CRM philosophy has been embraced, functional operations adjusted, and work processes reengineered, it's time to talk software and other tools because now you know exactly what you need. A developer doesn't decide what type of house to build based on the tools at his or her disposal. In the same vein, you shouldn't let the capability and nature of your software dictate the level of CRM success you plan to shoot for. Your customers should do that, and you should respond by finding the software that meets their needs.

But effective CRM will be the result of managing multiple operations in ways that not only enable and empower customers to have a more effective hand in their own purchasing destiny, but also combine and unite systems in ways that allow all information to be available to the necessary parties whenever they need it. Often, this is easier said than done.

Unless the company is brand new, it undoubtedly has some kind of legacy computer system that has evolved over time and sports the type of "spaghetti" architecture we all know and love that connects its various operational and departmental silos. Research has shown such siloed architecture costs roughly 30 percent more to build and maintain and results in a 30 percent greater lag time in executing functions and providing services. All in all, this is not a very CRM-friendly approach.

Under effective CRM, all systems integrate and every action affects every other related function. Thus, an enterprisewide approach needs to be implemented in order to effectively manage the process. Moreover, it must develop in a way that anticipates technology needs not only now but in the future to accommodate the inevitable growth your company will enjoy as a result of its CRM successes.

The complexities of such an effort, of course, can be staggering because it must include the following components:

- Web access and interaction that will help collect and synthesize customer data, as well as personalize responses to their inquiries and needs;
- Computer telephony integration software to track and integrate messages among various systems nodes and components;
- An operational customer database that sorts and segments customer information and transaction history across all channels of "contact," providing a single point of view and central information respository for access;
- Data-mining and information-routing capabilities to allow customer information to be accessed in ways meaningful to the needs of the company and enable that information to be shared throughout the network;
- Channel infrastructure engines that enable the access to and integration of Web information, e-mail, call center data and other resources;
- And undoubtedly a host of enablers, engines and other software applications.

This all falls under the heading of enterprise customer management, also known as ECM, and allows one-to-one customer customization on both incoming and outgoing contacts with customers. In addition to making data mined about the customer accessible, ECM systems log contact dates, information and responses that allow whomever is talking to or communicating with this person the ability to literally pick up where the company representative left off the last time contact was made. This goes a long way to supporting CRM because it keeps the customer from having to re-explain his or her issue each time. Moreover, it makes the customer feel not only like someone at the firm knows what's going on, but also that they care about the customer. That, of course, is central to developing long-term relationships, which, in turn, lies at the heart of CRM.

It's important to remember, too, that CRM systems are proactive in their pursuit of customer service, not just a better way to react to incoming calls. Strategies can be built around the new levels and types of information now available to customer service managers and reps. Targets can be better defined, customer segments can be more finely sorted. In the end, marketing and service efforts will improve simply because customer data is more readily available and more easily sorted and its results more successfully implemented.

Taking time to master the complex CRM equation will yield multiple benefits. But do it right the first time; that way, you won't have to do it again.

Chapter S5
Branding Your Internet Identity

Every product or service has an identity in the marketplace. Your product, your company and your Internet presence are no different.

Part of that identity is built on the qualities associated with that product or service, part is based on price. When we think of a pickup truck from Ford Motor Company, durability and reliability are two words that come to mind, as well as a competitive price within the marketplace for similar products. When we hear the phrase, "Intel Inside," we know that Andy Grove's strategy for the microprocessing giant once again has made the presence of Intel's component part critical in the minds of customers. We wouldn't have our desktop, laptop or palmtop any other way.

All of those characteristics are just that—characteristics. The pickup truck's durability and the microprocessor's critical functionality are features that lead to benefits associated with purchases of those products. They are part of, but not the heart of the brand that both products carry. But when it comes to truly identifying brand, there's more to the process than just features and benefits. Branding is both as simple and as complex as anything within your business's marketing function, which is where the combined concept and discipline lives. Brand your product, service, company or Web site successfully and fame and fortune can and will be yours.

Sound simple? It is...and it isn't. Whether we're talking about washing machines, wine cellars or Web sites, effective brand development is an elusive thing that doesn't miraculously occur just because a company has done all the right things and amassed all the right pieces. Brand is more than a logo and tagline; more than packaging and placement; it's even more than product and price. In fact, the gestalt of branding is all that. And more.

Michael Knapstein, chief executive officer of Waldbillig & Besteman, an advertising and marketing firm, describes brand as the consummation of the relationship between the product, the company and the customer. It's the promise made to the customer—be that the promise of flavor, color, quality or performance—and the delivery of that promise. The net return for the company is the loyalty the customer feels to that company and the willingness to purchase that product again and again. Even in an on-line world.

How much is brand loyalty worth? More than you can imagine. And the value of that brand goes from the obvious to the ephemeral.

Consider the Walt Disney brand. The empire founded by the one-time artist and animator has grown to be an entertainment conglomerate the scope of which its founder had never dreamed. In addition to animated shorts and features, the Disney brand has gone on to encompass other types of films, theme parks, consumer products, even cruise ships and clothing stores. Yet each and every manifestation of the brand comes with the assurance of high-quality, wholesome, family-based entertainment with educationally redeeming features and top-notch service on which parents and children of all ages can rely.

Disney presents an ironclad brand to its customers and enjoys fierce loyalty from those customers in return. That loyalty is so strong that the company is assured of a ready-made market, no matter what it produces and distributes. The brand itself is so strong, in fact, that its wealthier customers have gone to the next level of purchasing Disney stock to help ensure that the brand lasts forever, or at least until their own children and grandchildren have grown.

Brand is the relationship between your company and its customers, and that includes all support and peripheral devices, such as Web sites. If your Web site is not effectively supporting your firm's brand proposition, then it would be better if you didn't have a Web site at all.

Before Brand, Positioning

Chances are you already think you know what brand is. Microsoft is a brand, Coca-Cola is a brand, Taco Bell is a brand, right? Each of those companies has a well-recognized product, a place in the marketplace, an identity in the minds of consumers. Ergo, each is a successful brand, if only because we all know what the firm and its products represent.

That's certainly true, but they didn't arrive at brand status through divine intervention. Before they could become recognized as desirable household names, they first had to find their right place in the marketplace, a place where they could cultivate and grow the identity outlined by the senior management team, CEO, board of directors or, more likely, a combination thereof. And that's what's known as positioning.

Brand is the result of good positioning and good positioning always precedes effective brand development. That's one of the foundational laws of business and the first and foremost marketing commandment.

There are two types of positioning. Physical positioning describes the relationship of your product to other similar products. Think of it as a type of shelf space. Among soft drinks, Pepsico's relatively new Sierra Mist is positioned against 7Up because of its similar color and flavor, for example, but not against Coke. There might be crossovers in the market segment each serves, but the two categories are different enough so that the physical positioning is distinct.

More to the point, however, is the perceptual positioning your company or product has in the minds of consumers. What do Sierra Mist and Coke mean to potential customers? How do they perceive their value and position in the soft-drink hierarchy? What role do they play in the consumer's lifestyle? Several years ago Pepsico attempted to position its flagship brand as a breakfast drink, capitalizing on the habit some regular drinkers had of replacing morning cups of coffee with the caffeinated beverage. The strategy was distinctly different from Pepsi's normal positioning as a recreational soft drink and its success probably depends on what type of beverage you have sitting next to your keyboard when you sit down in the morning.

At the risk of belaboring this marketing mini-lesson, suffice it to say that positioning is a critical foundation to brand development. Whether your goal is to launch a business, a product or a Web site, lack of appropriate positioning and planning will exactly parallel the lack of success you can expect. All businesses—and especially e-businesses—need to consider their positioning before they can hope to achieve brand recognition. And brand recognition—especially of e-businesses—will be vital for future survival on-line where, truth be told, we really do all begin to look alike after awhile.

I hope I wasn't the first to tell you that. I'm sure I won't be the last.

DRILLDOWN

For the sake of both clarity and brevity, executives at Waldbillig & Besteman have developed a 10-step process to branding you may find useful as you approach development of a Web page "brand":

1. Develop a brand positioning statement that describes the company/product /Web site and its benefits in a language the consumer will understand.
2. Articulate a brand "vision" statement that describes how the company/product/Web site should be perceived in one, five and ten years.
3. Create a brand that uniquely expresses those positioning and vision statements.
4. In the same vein, create a brand phrase to express the primary customer benefit.
5. Develop a brand graphic mark or logo that distinctly expresses these characteristics.
6. Create a brand graphic identity or standard that supports both the logo and the benefit quality message to consumers.
7. Identify a brand communications style—tone of voice, copy approach—that does the same textually that the graphic identity does visually. Then use both consistently.
8. Develop brand equity, defined as a blend of all such components that establishes and holds a unique position within the marketplace.
9. Build a brand communications plan around these elements that can accomplish stated goals in a cost-effective manner.
10. Create a brand personality with which consumers can develop a relationship, the ultimate goal of brand development.

Developing Your Internet "Brand"

Volumes have been written on brand development, and volumes will be written on Internet brand development as the need for greater on-line differentiation continues to grow. Whether you credit the proliferation of Web sites, the growing Internet traffic, the need for on-line differentiation or the rocky promise of e-commerce success for this growth, it all adds up to a greater need to set yourself apart from the millions of other sites out there. And, given the fact that most Webcrawlers choose your site based on a half-dozen words of text coughed up by any of a half-dozen search engines, setting yourself apart and making your Web identity appealing is no easy task.

First things first, however, and that's understanding how the Internet functions as an information and marketing engine in the mind of the consumer. First and foremost, marketers will tell you, perception is reality. That means that how consumers perceive your company, your service and your Web site is how those things are in their minds. That gives life to these perceptions and makes them reality. It doesn't matter what your intentions are or were. It doesn't matter what you really did (well, not much anyway.) What matters is what your customers and the people who drift into your Web site believe you to be. That's why brand is so important.

Pick a product, a topic or an industry, then check out the related Web sites provided by your search engines. Splash pages pop up with more bells and whistles than the average circus calliope, eager to draw you in with bright colors, whirligig graphics and pointed marketing messages that tell you in no uncertain terms how their products whiten and brighten. If you're just looking for product information, chances are you'll click this monster off before it even finishes loading. Chances are, too, that none of these images have even registered on your radar screen, but the company sponsoring the page will never know that because your hit has been recorded and goes down in the logbook as a successful visit. Far from it, you say. If so, then let that be a lesson on branding your own page.

Before attempting to brand your Web site, brand your company and make sure your Web site reflects and supports that brand. If there is no integration between on-line and off-line strategies, there is no effective branding, period.

Remember, the Internet is the consummate form of direct marketing. It exceeds telemarketing in its immediacy and direct mail in its content and impact. But all Internet branding and marketing efforts must exist as part of the overall direct marketing strategy. When all is said and done, the Internet is merely one more medium—albeit the most profound and powerful medium—through which to interact with customers and the general public.

Part of what you'll need to communicate is clear identification and application of your product's or your company's brand. That's easily done over the Internet, which offers unlimited potential for the amount and type of information accessible, as well as site tools that allow interested consumers to explore at will and to whatever depth might be appropriate to their needs.

Remember, however, that in the on-line world, content is king and commerce is second. Good content often begets healthy commerce, but aggressive marketing not backed by valuable information tends to fall flat because Web users aren't yet used to seeing Web sites as marketing engines. That will change over time but, for now, it's best to be subtle and subversive in your on-line marketing efforts rather than risk the immediate turnoff that overcommercialized sites and "spam" e-mails can foster.

DRILLDOWN

E-mail can be an effective tool to get your brand message across as well, but the lists that you beg, borrow or steal need to be a reliable source of good names and e-mail addresses; otherwise your efforts will be wasted or worse. Opt-in e-mail lists, with names gathered from voluntary registrations on various appropriate Web sites, can be a good source. But there are cautions involved with these lists:

- Make sure the rental list truly is an opt-in list and that consumers have voluntarily added their names. If that isn't the case, then using the list will be a waste.

- Quality matters. If the list resulted simply from people signing up for free merchandise, chances are you have a hodgepodge of names, only some of which will be worthwhile. If, on the other hand, the list is the subscriber list to a free e-zine dedicated to the very topic in which you have an interest, the list could be worth its weight in gold.

- Needless to say, the length of the list and its sponsor are also determinants of quality. Whether the list can be sorted in a way that meets your marketing and branding needs also makes a difference.

- Remember that securing the list is just the first step. Research shows that it may take as many as five to seven contacts before list prospects will act on an offer. Once you have the list, use it wisely and well. Only then will you reap rewards.

Why Are You Here?

Marketing is a complex science based on sound customer research and designed to build relationships with consumers that will grow in share-of-wallet over time. Any marketer will tell you that and it is, indeed, true. But what that means in application is quite simple:

- Know your company and its products inside and out.
- Understand the nature of those products, their use and perceived value by customers.
- Recognize the value and application, including opportunities and restrictions, of the various media available to you to educate customers as to the benefits of those products.
- Combine all aspects into an effective sales pitch.
- Sit back and reap the rewards of your efforts.

Internet marketing can fit well into this equation, exerting a powerful impact on your Web site visitors. Once again, however, there are site opportunities and restrictions to observe in sharing your marketing message. Do that, however, and you'll have a greater chance of success than if you treated your Web site like any other medium.

What it all boils down to, of course, is positioning. That's the step that precedes branding and determines how the product/service/Web site is perceived by customers. Ask yourself the following questions:

- Does my Web site stand up to the competition in terms of accessibility, graphical sophistication, content and perceived value by customers? (This is physical positioning.)
- Does my Web site provide the level of value to customers comparable to their needs and the Web's availability to do so? Is my site content-rich or marketing-heavy? Can visitors make informed product decisions, or am I hoping to hypnotize them with hyperbole? Do they see a site that reflects the sophistication they expect from the company and its product line, or is the site painfully behind the times? (Success in these areas is the result of perceptual positioning.)

How successful you are in branding your site will depend, first, on how sophisticated your thinking is about the site and its true purposes and, second, on how your execution reflects that thought and planning. The site's ultimate marketing value—its return on investment, if you will—is the direct result of the other two characteristics.

First Steps

Once you grasp the nature of your positioning on your Internet site, developing brand becomes that much easier. The concept for on-line marketing is best spelled out as follows:

Information + Interactivity =
Consumer Interest/Involvement

A Web site identified for its ease of navigability and richness of content can be a brand unto itself. The fact that many e-commerce companies exist only on-line makes this even more critical to success. Finding a domain name that reflects the company and its brand while enabling current and potential customers to find you amid the noise and clutter of the Web is the real challenge.

Your domain name—the identifier by which users "log on" to your web site—should be reflective of your brand identity. This not only supports the brand but also allows consumers easier access because of their familiarity with your product. I might not remember the identity of the Mars Candy Company, but I will know enough to type in *www.snickers.com* if I want information on one of my favorite confections. That works best with product-focused firms. If, on the other hand, your brand development has focused on identifying the company—like United Airlines, for example—then the Web site should highlight the company name, initials or acronym—*www.UAL.com*.

This is a good way to test brand recognition, but be careful that it doesn't scuttle your on-line development efforts if your brand isn't as well known as you think it is. Using it as a domain name for your Web site in such cases might undermine development efforts on both sides. And don't get overly cute or obscure with your site name if it supports an existing product or firm. If you do, you may have to build brand identity for the firm separate from what you already may have done for your product or company. Some people are intrigued enough by unusually named sites to dial them up and take a look. Many more, however, simply want to find your site and get the information they need. Helping them cut down on their search time will help you reach more current and potential customers.

DRILLDOWN

When it comes to branding on the Internet, it may be as simple as having the right name in the right place and time. Company strategy and a domain name come first. Add a tag line and supporting logo graphic and, many firms feel, they're in business. The lesson here is a simple one: As vast as the resources of the Internet are, the opportunity for brand identification is conversely much simpler.

Think of the Nike "swoosh," Pepsi's red, white and blue "sphere," or any of a dozen car company emblems, from the distinctive H for Honda to the even more distinctive Mercedes Benz lines in a circle. Your Web site doesn't need to be overdone with colors, motion and graphics. It does need to be clean and accessible and have a memorable takeaway graphic symbol that can be used repeatedly and with immediate recognition. That will be integral to your Web site branding efforts.

Searching for the Right Search Engine

Making your Web site distinctive once users have logged on isn't as difficult as getting them to visit in the first place. Like any merchant, you want your site to have traffic but, like any smart merchant, you want your site to have the right traffic; visits from the people who are going to buy what you're selling. Part of that is identifying whether the company or product name is the bigger draw and then grabbing the right domain name and Internet Protocol identifier as appropriate. For big-name brands, it's often that simple.

Another strategy that helps build Web site traffic, thus supporting the brand, is better placement on the search engines of choice. Search engines are the key to success on the World Wide Web. Without them, in fact, there would be no Web. Strategically placing your Web site name near the front of lists resulting from searches of keywords will separate you from hundreds of would-be competitors, increasing Web site traffic, thus strengthening your on-line brand. No matter what you do up front, in fact, you'll find that it's a never-ending process.

First and foremost, you'll want to be listed on the top search engines currently cruising the Web. We'll talk a little more about that in Appendix D. Your site's log files will tell you which engines currently send you the most traffic. Cross-compare that traffic with customer records to see if those are reliable hits, or simply cyber window shoppers. Make sure, too, to check your page's position in the list generated by that site for specific searches. Are the right keywords driving you to the head of the list every time?

As for those other engines that haven't been quite as successful in driving customers to your site, what can be done to stimulate traffic? Do those other engines attract the same level of traffic as your site? How are you positioned in the ranking whenever anyone does a keyword search? Some investigation at your end may improve traffic—and, ultimately, sales—significantly.

Linkages to other, related sites may improve visitation to your site. Check out possibilities and look for products or services conceptually or operationally adjacent to yours. Today, cooperation exceeds competition as a strategic development tool. This is especially true on the Web. Take advantage of consumers' tendencies to check out hot links to other sites and make sure yours is a top choice among links. And despite what I just said, check the sites of your competition to see if they're doing anything that you're not to improve traffic as it relates to keyword searches.

Not all searches, all engines or all sites will rank things the same. Be realistic about what you can hope to accomplish. There are ways to improve activity, some of which are within your control. That won't be true in all cases, however. You can check keyword placement. You can use ALT tags for your graphic images, which will attract the attention of some search engines. You can use software that specializes in search engine optimization. All of these devices will be helpful, but none will attract all of the Webcrawlers all of the time. Like other media, the Web has its limits. If you can maximize your options within those limits, you will be much better off.

In the end, what makes an effective Web brand is what makes an effective brand overall:

- High-quality products or services that meet a designated or stated customer need;
- Excellent service consistently delivered in ways that meet or beat customer expectations, so the only surprises are good ones;
- Reliability in response to customer questions, comments or complaints, including timeliness and complete and thorough handling of any issues or problems;
- Follow-up and follow-through in all facets of operation; and
- Guarantees, premiums and other incentives that mean repeat business in the future, either on-line or through other methods.

Calvin Coolidge said the business of America is business. Today, he might have changed that to e-business, but not at the expense of business overall. Companies that define their strategies first, then plan their Web site as part of the follow-through, can be enormously successful. But as with everything else, technology alone is not a panacea for all business problems. Keep things in perspective and the brand your Web site carries will be as successful as your company can make it. No more, no less.

Chapter S6
The Extra Advantage of Extranets

Let's start out this chapter with a few definitions. In an industry cluttered with so much jargon, it's always good to sing from the same greenbar song sheet:

- INTERNET. Often mistakenly shorthanded as the World Wide Web, the Internet is the computer on-line network that links Netheads around the world. There is no charge for using the Internet and no restrictions keeping users from its wealth of connections and information. All you need is a personal computer, a modem, and access through an Internet Service provider (ISP). The Internet has single-handedly revolutionized the way we think, communicate and conduct business.

- INTRANET. Not to be confused with the Internet, an intranet uses the same Web technology to provide access and connectivity to a select group of users who have a specific interest or investment in an organization, company or firm. An intranet provides access for the on-line needs of the group located behind the firewall of said firm. This generally includes the employees and staff of a company or organization. Unlike the Internet, which is open to everyone, an intranet is a highly secure, Web-based network.

- EXTRANET. Think of an extranet as a combination of the above scenarios designed to provide access to specific users for specific purposes. Extranets are secure Web-based networks that exist beyond the firewall of a company, organization or firm and provide subscribers with access to specific information for specific reasons. Whereas intranets are generally limited to employees, extranets extend the same access to suppliers, business partners, vendors, consultants and anyone else outside the immediate on-line family who needs access to privileged company information.

- SECURENET. This is simply another name for an extranet that passes the necessary security and encryption tests so that proprietary information may pass over the Web without falling into the hands of your competition, cybercrooks, and other assorted bad persons. In order to exist and operate, an extranet must also be a securenet; otherwise, it has no reason to exist and may do more harm than good.

What none of the above definitions tell you is the fact that, like the Internet before it and more so than any intranet, today's extranets are revolutionizing the way we do business. A good extranet combines the best of both Nets to create a business-to-business environment that is dynamic and immediate and that solves problems and addresses issues in real time. It handles queries, questions, orders and deliveries faster, more effectively and cheaper than any other medium or method. What the Internet did for the public at large extranets will do for the world's businesses. And, like the Internet, it will no longer be a matter of whether or not your company participates, but when and to what degree. Otherwise, the competition will leave you in its cyber dust.

And that doesn't even take into account the question of portals. And neither will we, at least not until Chapter S7.

DRILLDOWN

In terms of protocols, all extranets operate much the same. However, the terminology might be different. Certain European markets don't use the term extranet. Instead, they promote the use of "vertical Internets," which operate much the same, using Internet protocols and secured sites to serve a specific— or "vertical"—market of suppliers, vendors, partners and consultants.

No matter what the name, however, the outcome is still the same. The Gartner Group estimates that $17 billion in trading and sales currently pass through European vertical Internets. That number is expected to top $1 trillion by 2004 and will represent 13 percent of all European commerce conducted on the Web.

You Say You Want an Evolution

Despite what dyed-in-the-wool propellerheads may think, the extranet didn't develop just because someone found out how to do it and thought it would be cool. Like everything else, the need for extranets grew out of a sound business reason. In this case, that reason was the rapid-fire growth of service outsourcing.

Throughout the 1990s companies of all sizes, makes and models began to examine their operations and focus on core competencies. Some of those initiatives grew out of the old-fashioned stick-to-your-knitting mentality of long-time successful companies who found themselves diversified beyond their ability to cope with the scope of their own growth. Still more of it came about thanks to entrepreneurial firms still riding the roller coaster of their start-up phases, never knowing from month to month what staffing levels they needed to hit to service clients they may or may not have by the next quarter.

Across both these types of companies lay the glowing patina of improved customer service, total quality management and other philosophies du jour that bullied companies to stress what they do best and eschew all the rest. In short, no matter who you were, you were getting heavily into the outsourcing of extraneous or support services. Otherwise, chances are you were watching your net margin flounder under the ungainly weight of rapidly increasing overhead. For times demanding lean and mean operations, flaccid, expense-generating departments struggling to keep up the pace were not a pretty sight.

What outsourcing did do was free up capital, otherwise occupied with supporting those non-revenue–generating operations, to allow firms to compete more effectively. Whether those extra funds were plowed into additional marketing, research or product development, or simply reduced the need to borrow, which further reduced the squeeze on funds, outsourcing proved to be an effective answer and welcome respite to unwise growth.

In addition, the more entrepreneurially minded specialists, who may have been downsized out of their employment positions precisely because of the growing outsourcing phenomenon, found themselves with more opportunity and income than they could handle in the precise area in which they were most capable. For many supplier and buyer firms, things couldn't have been better.

At the same time, technology was racing ahead and the question remained how these outsource firms, no longer mere vendors but now considered operational partners, could interact with sometimes intimate aspects of operations and still manage to capitalize on the economies of scale. Could something as sensitive as managing payroll and benefits, for example, be outsourced while still allowing for the process to be done electronically and the results communicated over the wires on a regular basis without compromising the integrity of the data?

Enter the extranet. Its capabilities allowed companies to create shared and secure information links with vendor-partners and other critical components in their newly refined operational chains. Its facile nature also supports such things as just-in-time delivery of products and services, reduced inventory and warehouse demands, real-time consultation when it's needed, and a wide array of other assorted operational and competitive advantages. Once a company's extranet was in place, the rest became easy.

DRILLDOWN

For all the brouhaha about the revenue that can be generated and expenses saved, a basic extranet is relatively easy and cheap to set up and maintain. It's really no more than a piggyback channel attached to the ubiquitous Internet that is wrapped in security protocols. (More about that later.) Once inside the company firewall, basic Web browser technology, already in place, is all anyone should need.

The key challenge is getting vendor-partners and company staff to understand and use an extranet to its fullest degree. The State of Wisconsin Department of Administration, responsible for managing all state government construction projects, has a very simple solution. Builders who are not Web-savvy and ready to use the state's secured extranet feature aren't able to bid on projects because that's the only method by which bids may be submitted. If that's not an incentive to get on-line, then there isn't one.

Strategies and Applications

Extranets have already proven their worth as fast, flexible and effective tools for the companies that use them and the vendors that link to them. Like anything else, they are controlled by IT but don't exist as an IT function. Simply put, IT can manage an extranet, but if the company is not committed to exploring and developing its use, then it will have little value to the firm. This means support and involvement from both a top-down and a bottom-up approach in order to get the best possible use out of the network.

Moreover, extranets tend to be a holistic technology with linkages between individuals and among departments. Inventory control linked to suppliers through an extranet, for example, impact not only the warehouse, but shipping and receiving, sales and marketing, finance and accounting and a host of other functions along the supply and distribution chain that runs within the company. Failure of the entire firm to embrace the technology—and that means support from the corner office as well—will mean failure of the technology.

That failure will have a tremendous impact in terms of the company's bottom line. Extranet technology is big business and contributes largely to increased revenue and decreased expenditures in company operations. It's not something any company of any size can afford to ignore any longer.

Business-to-business Internet transactions are on a steep growth curve and will continue at a rapid rate as technology improves, costs go down and extranets become the preferred method to do business. According to Forrester Research, Internet-based commerce totaled $43.1 billion in 1998. Experts at the Cambridge, Massachusetts technology think tank estimate those numbers could grow to $1.3 trillion by 2003. During that same time period, Forrester says the Internet share of e-commerce equals 78 percent of the total dollar value spent in '98. Extranet relationships are playing key roles in driving that commerce to a fever pitch.

That's a pretty significant commerce stream. In addition, on-line relationships also offer significant savings through the automation of product and service delivery. Cisco Systems, a networking equipment supplier, reports that it books roughly $11 million in orders from resellers over the Web daily. The firm also saved nearly $363 million in 1998 alone in marketing, distribution and support costs because its extranet capabilities allowed it to hire that many fewer people to answer questions and assist customers. Those types of cost savings alone make extranets a good value.

Even without such data at your fingertips, good common business sense tells you that extranets can be utilized with key customers and in primary vendor relationships. Remember the 80/20 rule? The old axiom that a company gets 80 percent of its business from 20 percent of its customers is as valid in the cyber world as it was before the advent of on-line commerce. Allowing those customers extra special access through password-protected extranet services will promote increased business from customers you already have. That's where the money begins to multiply exponentially.

As long as we're dwelling on the customer side of the equation, let's consider other ways to maximize the technology:

- Tracking orders and deliveries helps improve customer relations by allowing them to know exactly where their shipment is at any given time. The contracts for this book, for example, were shipped to me via commercial carrier and mysteriously misrouted. A quick check by staff at Learning Network Direct, Inc. enabled the package to be found and rerouted back to the original destination. For my purposes, that was a critical slip-up that needed and received immediate reconciliation.

- Similar to the above situation, but in more of a preemptive style, project timelines can be established and updated on a regular basis. Those who have access to the Net site can check progress and communicate with those responsible around the clock, if need be, in order to meet those deadlines and accomplish tasks.

- The extranet can be used to make special offers and savings opportunities available to your customers. The United Airlines extranet offers special fares, contests and other incentives to its most frequent flyers. In addition to offering customers exclusivity, UAL can control the impact of its offers and end them at a moment's notice once quotas and goals are filled.

- One of the most popular new features is the on-line newsletter, or e-zine, delivered over extranets to interested subscribers. The best ones are interactive, which means a certain level of security is critical. Extranets can and do provide that, giving the e-zine publisher the opportunity to get up close and personal without threatening the security of the relationship.

- Archival access may be one of the best uses of an extranet. By allowing interested and involved parties access to company documents and records, you are able to facilitate many processes that otherwise would have required face-to-face meetings or courier services. Once again, the security of an extranet makes a big difference.

- In the same vein, business and contractual processes can be facilitated over an extranet. A design and construction firm we know carried on meeting and approval processes for a major project with a client across town without sitting down together more than once or twice. The firm estimates that the on-line extranet-based relationship saved them weeks of time and tens of thousands of dollars in staff time and costs for meetings that never had to take place.

There are other uses and a wealth of industries that can benefit from the technology. Purchasing, distribution, inventory management and other tasks that involve cataloging and transporting merchandise are obvious tasks that come to mind. But more firms are also using it as a management and administrative tool with great success. Contracts can be shipped, reports and meeting minutes shared and cybervotes taken over extranets. It's all just a matter of how creative and insightful you can be in applying its uses.

DRILLDOWN

If your company is still behind the extranet curve, don't fret. Despite the growing demand for secure access, experts agree that most industries will see only incremental growth in extranet applications over the next few years. Many companies don't even know what an extranet is, while others are loath to allow on-line secure access to critical files, information and portals for those not on the company payroll. Once it's clear how the technology can lower transaction costs and improve service, executives will start singing a different tune.

Part of the reluctance may be sticker shock over the price of a complex, comprehensive system. While the basics are easy to set, truly interactive capabilities involving global customer access can cost anywhere from $100,000 to $1 million to purchase, install and facilitate, depending on how large and extensive a network you want to operate. Starting small, with a few key users that provide critical services connected to the main office is often the best way to start.

Feeling Secure

No matter what their intended and realized operational advantage, of course, extranets will never become the business-to-business exchange medium of choice unless both parties are confident about the system's security protocols. Security is the cornerstone of extranet success. Without it, the ability to utilize the technology would not be available and the methodology could not exist.

We started this chapter by identifying the need for secure Nets. Understanding and appreciating this aspect will be the single greatest factor to developing a system that is truly effective.

Such concerns have their seeds, of course, in early horror stories of hackers who toppled firewalls and decoded poorly encrypted transmissions, running away with hundreds of credit card numbers and PINs and creating economic havoc for companies and consumers alike. The possibilities still exist, of course, for wholesale mishaps to occur. Despite what we'd like to believe, they always will. For every security measure put into place, there's an enterprising cybercrook attempting to crack it. This game of leapfrog will continue, but the good news is that company IT departments are making great strides in protecting critical commercial data.

In a B2B extranet, this need takes on added dimensions. In addition to commercial exchange information, such as credit card numbers, there also are critical business and contractual documents that are subject to hacking, presenting firms with even greater risks than mere financial assaults. B2B enterprise has raised the stakes, and the need for added security right along with them.

Each company must take its own security steps, ever mindful of the nature and depth of liabilities that can be invoked against it for failing to protect critical information. Fortunately, the industry has ramped up its standard operating procedures, which have answered many of the security questions that already have been raised.

Much of the problem, industry experts say, has to do with scalability. Security protocols that have worked for a controlled number and groups of users now have to be adapt to meet the needs not of thousands but, in many cases, millions of on-line users. Consider how the challenges faced by a company seeking to maintain a secure extranet with a small group of vendors and consultants compare to those faced by a large on-line retailer like Amazon. com and you will begin to understand the issues at hand.

There are a number of security options, each of which has its advantages and disadvantages. Here's a selection of the most viable solutions:

- The need for names, passwords, digital certificates and other secret decoder ring-type devices is a given, of course. User authentication and authorization will be the first step to on-line security and maintenance of data integrity. This requires commitment on both sides to keep confidential data out of the general populace. A public/private key infrastructure (PKI) is an essential component that will take this to the next level, a vital component for business-to-business users for whom the keying of password and name may not only appear rudimentary and cumbersome, but also signal an unsophisticated system that may be easily cracked.

- Secure socket layers (SSLs) offer very good encryption methodologies that can be especially applicable for consumer-based credit card sales. Encrypted data by itself is another credit security component; its transmission through SSLs is something many companies have undertaken. The technology's major drawback is that its data management needs make it very server-intensive. You'll need a lot of horsepower to manage and run an effective SSL. In some cases, that won't be a problem; in others, however, that could mean a significant upgrade in your current system. When figured against the revenue-enhancing and cost-saving nature of an extranet, an investment in the tens of thousands that could yield an increased net margin in the millions might not be such a bad investment. SSLs also need to come equipped with a PKI, which could add a layer of operational bureaucracy. Once again, however, the value gained from having to maintain that level should far outweigh the cost and relative inconvenience of such a bureaucracy.

- For the sake of business-to-business commerce, virtual private networks (VPNs) might have more appeal to users. The protocol, also known as "tunneling," creates a private data stream delivered across a public communications channel, for example, a tunnel that is protected from the general audience and limited only to its senders and receivers. Basically, this involves developing individual Internet protocol packages and tucking them inside encrypted ones to preserve the integrity of the enclosed information. If you can't "see" through the outside bag, developers say, you won't be able to see into the inside bag.

- Tunneling can be developed through the use of two protocols: point-to-point tunneling protocol (PPTP), which also includes its derivative, layer 2 tunneling protocol, or L2TP; and IP Security protocol, also known as IPSec. PTPP can be very effective in connecting millions of users or simply two routers, despite that fact that it's a nonstandard protocol. Steps are being taken to make L2TP standard, another benefit to what already is a critical strength. L2TP is a layer 2 protocol that already supports many of the existing technologies. Its capability to seamlessly support security technologies helps it come closer to standard than PPTP.

- Despite that fact that many users prefer PPTP/L2TP to IPSec, L2TP relies on IPSec standards for encryption. Generally speaking, IPSec is better at this step because it contains an integrity check to make sure the data stream you said you sent is the data stream the party at the other end really received, while also performing key exchanges. IPSec supports a variety of encryption programs including DES, IDEA and others and comes closer to standard than the other protocols, a factor that helps manage the algorithm defaults during each communication. If PPTP is a tactical tool, then IPSec has a great likelihood of catching and perhaps even surpassing its capabilities at some point.

One of the key points that many companies fail to realize, however, is that security isn't only about encryption, passwords, firewalls and having the right software and language protocols in place. In the same way that CRM does not start with software, extranet security is not only a matter of system capabilities. Security begins with management and controlling not only how the information goes over the wires, but what information is appropriate to send. Taking unnecessary risks, despite software security capabilities, is bad policy no matter how you look at it.

While single directories managing senders and receivers on both sides of the firewall are critical, sufficient policy to manage the nature and extent of the information sent can help make that fortress even more impregnable. Here are some thoughts on migrating extranet security to the next phase:

- Systems should be broadly accessible within company-defined risk standards inside the firewall. This will increase use, acceptance and support by staff and executives, minimizing the need for exceptions and, along with it, additional security risks. Inclusion rather than exclusion should be the corporate mandate.
- Make the security infrastructure invisible. By drawing less attention to it, you will keep would-be hackers from realizing the depth and breadth of the system. It's the opposite of posting signs boasting of security systems on your house and more like the invisible fencing used in some neighborhoods to keep pets in the yard and unwanted strays out.
- Build your system around authentication, authorization and accountability. Make sure only those you desire to gain entry may pass through the shield; monitor their presence and activity; and make them accountable

for their actions while they're in your yard. That way, your system is based less on mechanical actions and more on intrinsic and intuitive responses. You'll not only control the flow at the entry point but stand to gain a wealth of information as users move through your system. And who could ask for more than that?

DRILLDOWN

Se habla español? More importantly, does your extranet speak Spanish? Consultants say that if you're doing business internationally, your software better be multilingual if you're planning to make points with your foreign clients and partners. According to Click Interactive, a Chicago-based software developer, companies doing business in the Western Hemisphere had better be prepared to speak English, Spanish, French and Portuguese while on-line. Canadians doing business in Vancouver, B.C., may also want to brush up on their Asian languages.

If you're doing business in Europe, it's helpful to be able to respond in Danish, Dutch, English, French, German, Italian, Norwegian and Swedish. At this point, you don't even want to think about the rest of the world.

Chapter S7

Not Just Any Portal in the Information Storm

A few years back, the Web world was running amok with what some said was a radical approach to data management, a new and improved way to handle the increasing flurry of factoids and flow of information that were inundating all users. From now on, the seers said, we're all going to bow to the new way of thinking and sharing called "portals."

New way of thinking, indeed. Portals in their purest form have been a long-standing operations methodology on the World Wide Web all the way back to CompuServ's early attempts at building what are now fondly called on-line "communities." Portals have been the focal point of many e-businesses since their conception. Companies like Amazon.com couldn't exist without them.

What is new, however, is a renewed interest in portal applications for controlled audience segments, internal information transmission within companies and, especially, in e-commerce applications. Portals certainly aren't new; however, newly refined uses for them are being discovered. Now when it comes to commerce and management strategies, portals have become big e-business. If your company doesn't have one now, rest assured it probably will soon. And you may not even know the difference.

In some ways, portals function similarly to the intranets and extranets discussed in Chapter S6. They provide on-line access to information for both broad audiences as well as specialized information to specific clientele, usually folks working in the same business. Yahoo!, Lycos and AOL are among the best-known portals serving the general Web-happy public. The human resource benefits network for employees of St. Louis brewer Anheuser-Busch, however, is a very different kind of portal, one destined to serve the specific needs of a specific audience. At a glance, there is similarity among the more common Net navigational engines. You've seen it all before.

But there is one big difference. In an on-line world drowning in data and awash in informational effluvia, where users have become sick of wading through a sea of chaff for an occasional nugget of wheat, portals are the floodgates that control the flow. They can be customized to fit personal needs and they can limit, organize and sort the sea of data. And that's a value that can't be denied.

Prosaically speaking, the dictionary defines "portals" as points of entry, doorways that admit or restrict access to whatever is on the other side. That's also what Web portals do. They perform a similar task by imposing a structure on data and a navigation scheme through the informational seas, resulting in greater management capabilities that help turn that data into information and that information into knowledge for the user. Intranets and extranets provide an aggregation of knowledge opportunities. They're still critical links in the chain. Portals offer a methodology by which those aggregations can be efficiently accessed based on the needs of those users. When it comes to business portals, that's a factor crucial to continued Web capabilities.

For the chief technology officer of a large corporation or organization, it's not whether his of her firm needs a portal. Rather, the question is how that portal can be introduced and implemented quickly, cleanly and to the greatest effect. Resources are great to have, but if you can't find your way around the vast Web library, then they won't do you much good.

DRILLDOWN

Portals have been around in one form or another since AOL and CompuServe began to battle for market dominance in the 1980s. The proliferation of enterprise, or corporate, portals is offset by the pending consolidation of public portals as the leaders grow in size, shape and influence. Size of customer base and portal adaptability have proven to be key factors in survival.

Industry watchers predict current leaders AOL, Yahoo! and Excite will all survive the inevitable shakeout. Thanks to deep pockets and strategic investment, Microsoft will also likely float to the top, followed by relative newcomers Disney/InfoSeek and NBC/Snap. All agree, however, that consolidations will continue until perhaps as few as three and as many as five public portals remain.

Coming of Age

The race to "portalize" the Web environment is the product of many things, not the least of which is the need for better access to more refined, well-sorted information. Data's increasing use as a management tool is another reason for the upswing. Since portals tie directly into the Internet, as well as the plethora of intra- and extranets out there, portal application and development is aided by already having a distribution avenue in place.

One of the most critical aspects, however, once again has to do with the Web's need to create better access to niche markets, not only for information purposes, but also for advertising. More and more, commerce is moving to the Web. In the case of business-to-business enterprise, the rapid pace of that movement is almost mind-numbing. Being able to tap niches within that market in a commercially meaningful way could mean astounding success in what is truly becoming the hottest and fastest-growing mass media on the planet.

But tapping the potential is not without its challenges, and savvy advertisers know that who you reach is as important as how many you reach, if not more so. And when you can reach the largest possible number of the best possible audience members, then you have the best of both worlds.

Think about it for a moment in terms of the product or service you market or sell. With its long-standing market dominance, Yahoo! is probably the most significant portal on the planet. Nearly 70 million people click on Yahoo! each month. Somewhere in the mass of international humanity is the core audience for your product or service. Through Yahoo! and other existing portals, you can reach them in a way that may or may not be relevant to them as consumers. And the number of people who aren't interested in what you're peddling will simply ignore your Web banner.

More simply put, the cost-per-thousand—advertising lingo for how much each set of eyeballs that falls on your marketing message is worth—may indeed be economical considering the reach. However, the value to you as an advertiser for reaching a whole lot of people for which you have no use...well, that's another question entirely.

More niche-oriented portals are the answer. Some advertisers refer to these as vertical portals or "vortals," windows to narrowly defined market segments that provide the type of action-oriented audience of consumers most advertisers seek for their products. In fact, research has shown that, in general, advertisers spend two-thirds of their ad dollars on vortal placement, compared to one-third on general all-purpose Web access windows. More and more of them, it seems, are recognizing this same value proposition.

The dichotomy in that equation is further enhanced by the difference in price between the two. A general run-of-site placement might cost an advertiser as little as $2 per CPM, whereas a highly tailored vortal ad could run as much as $200 per placement. For most advertisers, it's not a question of cost so much as it is of value. Advertising vintage Corvette parts on AOL, for example, will no doubt bring in some trade. Running a banner on a sports car enthusiasts' vortal, on the other hand, will significantly increase both the perception and the business realized by that company. The value of the vortal is far greater than the cost would indicate. Clickthrough rates alone bear this out.

The fact that money is a driving factor in portal and vortal development comes as no surprise given the mass migration to the Web and the financial impact of that migration. Web tracker Jupiter Communications estimates that Web site ad revenues will have grown from $940 million in 1997 to more than $8 billion in 2002. Of that amount, the Big 3—Yahoo!, AOL and MSN—are estimated to have grabbed 15 percent of the Internet traffic and 45 percent of on-line ad revenue. And if that's not enough to make even the most recalcitrant advertiser sit up and take notice, Forrester Research reports that vortals will attract 57 percent of Net advertising by the year 2004.

In the same way advertising has supported and, in some cases, driven publication creation in the print world, those forces likely will be brought to bear in the development of vertical portals. There may not yet be a vertical portal for Spanish-speaking, backpacking mothers-to-be, but give it time. The market is sure to come around.

DRILLDOWN

Enterprise portals, those committed to a single company or organization, present a wide variety of management and strategic information gleaned from sources throughout the enterprise, usually portrayed as small snapshots on a general Web page of opportunities and services. Those snapshots are made available through a technology called "portlets," which sound like something you might find at the butcher shop.

In reality, portlets are stand-alone presentations that can be combined, configured and presented on the general Web page. They serve as a gateway to additional information. Portlets also facilitate the customization that makes portals both appealing and more applicable to setting default values and creating preferences that help create, modify, manage and store personalized data.

An Enterprising Alternative

The advantages that portals like Yahoo! have brought to the burgeoning Web can't be denied, but a lot of companies are ready to move to the next stage, one in which they have a direct say in what is and isn't included and accessible to their employees. Besides, with a little more effort on their IT department's part, what has worked in the past for their customers is bound to work even better for them.

Such thinking led to the development of enterprise portals, also known as corporate portals. In the same way portals offer access and the ability to serve different market segments, the enterprise portal meets the same needs for companies and their employees and, if appropriate, consultants, vendors and other business partners. It's the best way to sort specific information and make it available in ways that make sense to the development and management needs of the enterprise through a single access point that combines the capabilities of existing legacy systems with new applications for increased and more easily accessed communications. This, in turn, contributes to the company's ability to operate more effectively in external e-business environments. But more on that later.

As mentioned earlier, successful enterprise portals tend to build on top of existing intranets and are built from the applications, documents and other data found in various departments from around the company. Good ones can cull Internet data, incorporate e-mail lists and integrate calendars and other operational data into a single start-up page that allows the user access to complete information. By taking a proactive approach, displaying the day's activities to those who log in and offering drilldown capabilities for those who seek more information, the enterprise portal can be customized to enhance productivity and stimulate action.

In short, a good enterprise portal can save staff hours and employee efforts in terms of getting information, ideas, directives and thoughts together before getting their day going. Multiply the time saved across an organization with a thousand or more employees and suddenly that effort seems more than merely just a good idea. It becomes downright critical to increased productivity and staff effectiveness.

The ability to customize the portal to personal needs within the company makes the whole concept even more intriguing. Consider for a moment the average corporate executive team. All members need basic knowledge of mission, vision, strategies and goals presented in much the same way and with the same emphasis so that they can direct their respective operations from the same level of understanding. Divisions and diversity in this level of understanding can undermine company efforts. The ability to stratify this information at a certain management tier level is a valuable benefit of corporate portals.

But that same group also needs information specific to the operational needs of the functions they supervise. The chief financial officer does not need to know the same industry trends and operating information as the marketing vice president, for example. To have to wade through that data is a waste of the CFO's time and energies. In this case, each of those individual's portals can be tailored so critical knowledge is immediately available at the click of the button. In that way, both levels of their professional needs are met in ways that provide consistency as well as custom tailoring to meet their specific requirements.

This data extends in a variety of areas as well. We've already touched on two critical needs for the executive-level management team. Personal business needs such as calendars, task lists and professional training tools are other things that can be included in the suite of services. Collaborative tools and access to legacy system processes can be adapted as other possible services. As long as the data can be delivered on-line, is relevant to the individual receiving it and fits with company goals and mission, it's fair game for any executive information portal.

How It All Works

Portal operations rely on an application platform that connects the necessary user interface capabilities of the individual portals. An application server powers the platform's connectivity. This enables the inclusion of critical features such as failover, load balancing, scalability, security, systems management and transaction capabilities, many of which are gained from the portal itself. All of these capabilities play into the business processes that run the system and emanate from the platform itself. This is also the operational layer to which new processes and enterprises will be added as the portal system progresses and matures.

The portal process may best be viewed as a series of steps tied to a strategic goal that is executed over a period of time as goals and resources warrant. Business rules and logic apply and their application usually drives portal development. Implementation of that logic, in fact, helps develop portal structure and govern the type and breadth of the information involved. If the enterprise system is well constructed, rules should be able to guide the structure without having to change application codes. Portals can and should be created to facilitate the storage and use of such rules.

The final step is application integration, which is generally accomplished through an integration server and a set of pluggable adapters, each of which is specific to whatever system it integrates into the whole. Adapters communicate with the appropriate external system and translate data from format to format. The integration server provides the necessary run-time environment and interfaces between the adapter-led external systems as a business process running the operations platform. Through this method, those systems linked by the adapters can be accessed through the portal and other existing operational systems.

DRILLDOWN

The earliest enterprise portals tended to focus on company human resource functions, using their capabilities to communicate policies, procedures, forms and mundane information such as holiday schedules. Much of it was the equivalent of internal brochureware. Once the information gateway was established, however, interactive applications soon followed. Those forms could be completed and e-mailed back to HR and employees were able to monitor and contribute to their own HR information. Other information and, eventually, other departments followed shortly thereafter.

Tapping the Reservoir

For some companies, it may be a relatively new concept, for others mere common sense, but it has become a central rationale for establishing enterprise portals: Part of any company's accrued value in the marketplace is the wealth of data and level of expertise contained within its walls. It's part of the talents, tools and value they bring as an enterprise to the marketplace. Good portals provide access to that information companywide. They also serve as a repository of self-management tools to help improve productivity. In their highest iteration, however, they also serve to synthesize these elements into a third tier of application, making the expertise, knowledge base and talents of all available to others in meaningful and highly applicable ways.

This goes a long way to justify enterprise portals' return on investment which, for many companies interested in setting up such a system, could be significant. Presumably the necessary hardware already is in place. Currently, portal software packages cost anywhere from $50,000 to $500,000. And that doesn't include the staff needed to manage the operation, refresh the necessary on-line information on a daily basis and, if need be, digitize documents and other information critical to increased productivity. Under such a potentially expensive scenario, the ROI would have to be fairly significant.

Formal synthesis into making your portal the ultimate management tool could make this all worthwhile, however. Surely there are other data repositories within your firm and other ways to schedule meetings and business lunches. There may even be good enough rapport among management team members so that sharing of ideas occurs on a fairly regular basis, perhaps even at a high enough level to make the efforts worthwhile. But a true synthesis of information and expertise, available to all, offers a level of insight and application not available through any other means. That's where the portal begins to pay for itself and produce ROI worth the effort of conceptualization and implementation.

Realize, of course, that you won't come across any out-of-the-box or off-the-shelf portal development packages that will plug in and turn on. Each company's needs are too specialized for such mundane applications. That means time, effort and expense to get your enterprise portal up and running. But, to paraphrase an old adage, if you find the cost of knowledge management to be too expensive, consider the corresponding cost of ignorance.

DRILLDOWN

Portals also can be used to link interested parties outside the firewall, allowing them access to information and interactivity in a way that facilitates productivity, revenue enhancement and cost savings. Supplier portals tend to be the most popular, with special emphasis on linking vendors to information, inventory and policy resources to facilitate their commercial exchange with the host company. Sometimes it's merely an information-sharing methodology; at other times it's an ordering mechanism. It all depends on how important a strategic tool the company sees its portal to be.

Beyond Mere Technology

The real key to making enterprise portal technology a worthwhile investment comes in linking it to strategy. Some technology is appropriate as part of the company's electronic toolbox or as an operational overlay. In the case of portal technology, however, the power and strength behind the portal lies in its personal applications. Having access to tools means little unless those tools are used to the fullest. That means your enterprise portal needs to be part of an overall strategy that not only utilizes the information present, but relies on the power of the portal to realize corporate goals. That means close ties to the company's strategic platform are not only desirable, but critical.

The company that moves in such a direction will be joining good company. A 1999 study by the Delphi Group showed that 55 percent of organizations surveyed already were operating in a portal environment. The same survey predicted that by 2002, nearly 90 percent of all organizations will have some level of enterprise portals up and running, an increase of close to 100 percent.

More to the point, perhaps, was the response in terms of personal preference. More than 60 percent of respondents indicated that they saw the corporate portal as a new "dashboard" capable of helping them better manage their rapidly diversifying workload. The majority of those saw it as supplanting or replacing the existing Windows-based environment that populates corporate desktops.

Such a point of view offers profound commentary on the nature, strength and ultimate impact of enterprise portals as the interface tool of choice within companies of all sizes. Those who talk about portals do so in terms not of information access, but of knowledge management.

Note the difference in the two terms. It is profound in the volumes it speaks about enterprise portals and their imminent applications.

Chapter S8
VOIP Is Not a Four-letter Word

The Internet is a marvelous medium, isn't it? It can carry text, pictures, even movies. You can get up-to-the-minute news and weather information for any city in the world, order your favorite pair of slacks from Eddie Bauer or your favorite lingerie from Victoria's Secret, even fill out a loan form to buy a car. In some markets, you can even print your own airline and event tickets so you don't have to wait on line for them.

What the Internet can't do quite as well is facilitate the average, banal telephone conversation—the kind you now have on that $19.95 phone you picked up at the local discount store—in real time. In other words, you can find out weather information from an empirical source, but you can't chat about it. "The weather in Moscow is 20 degrees Celsius," is information more easily shared, while "Hot enough for ya?" is a question less easily asked, at least on line.

This is changing thanks to inroads made by the continued advancement of voice-over-Internet protocols, known variously as voice-over IP or, simply, VOIP. With an eye toward saving money on long-distance charges and/or aggregating various information transmission resources into one medium, the corporate world has been watching and waiting for VOIP to come of age. If we can put men on the moon, they reason, there must be a way to let us talk to anyone anywhere in the world for the price of a local telephone call through the Internet.

For a long time, of course, this fell into the category marked "Works better in concept than in practice." But it's coming along and soon likely will be as common as a telemarketer, but not nearly as annoying.

> ### DRILLDOWN
>
> How much savings might a company realize by going to a voice-over IP environment? How many stars are in the sky? Various studies have turned up the following rather alarming statistics:
>
> - The average Fortune 500 company spends between $15 million and $20 million on telecommunications each year. Of that, 36 percent is used merely for faxing.
>
> - There are 60 million fax machines worldwide, accounting for $80 billion in telecommunications charges.
>
> That makes quite a case for VOIP as well as for fax-over-Internet protocols, also known as FOIP.

Ready, Set, Wait!

The origins of today's VOIP are generally traceable to 1995. That was when VocalTec Communications introduced some the earliest Internet telephone software designed to run on a 486 personal computer that had been outfitted with microphone, modem, speakers and a sound card. Other enabling software, such as Intel's own Internet Phone and NetSpeak Corporation's WebPhone, joined the emerging trend. Better sound cards, more effective compressions and greater modem speed all aided in the technology's development.

The biggest boost, however, was sociological rather than technical. As more and more employees joined the telecommuter ranks and began working from their homes, the need for economical communications grew. The ability to aggregate voice and data transmissions into one cost-effective (read: cheap) medium made a lot more financial sense to companies than to argue about reimbursable telephone calls to supposed clients who really turned out to be Aunt Martha in Poughkeepsie. What started out as a quirky little trick for Internet hobbyists quickly escalated to a practical application with sound business reasoning.

The concept and execution weren't as difficult as other, more common computer operations. The process is software driven, enabling the users' PCs to detect sound cards and modems at each end. (Just like a telephone, obviously, it takes two fully equipped and linked PCs to dance to this tango, too.) The setup procedures also included determining whether the call is half- or full-duplex and whether the IP address is static or changes with each log-on.

Voice data is then compressed into packets through a codec algorithm encoded through a compression modem. The "call" is then sent and decoded at the other end.

The problem—similar to that sometimes experienced with overseas telephone calling—is the latency period between information reception, decoding and dissemination. In other words, that annoying little delay that sometimes interrupts long-distance conversations and frustrates callers can be maddeningly magnified as the computer does its coding-and-decoding thing.

That, in fact, is the most difficult step in managing and implementing the technology. In order to maintain the quality of service (QOS) demanded by today's users and, probably, tomorrow's regulatory agency, voice-enabled networks have to maintain a one-way delay time of less than 300 milliseconds. This time period must include not only the time it takes to transmit the signal, but also encoding and decoding procedures and any delays caused by network configuration and transmission issues.

Those who study these things in depth say that encoding and decoding can take as little as 1 millisecond, while looping from PC to the local router at both ends may take 5 milliseconds each, with an additional 80 milliseconds for the call to make its cross-country journey. That leaves 208 milliseconds for the system to cope with the rigors of the network and hurdle any obstacles that might be in the way. Sometimes, that's enough; at other times, it's not. When those parameters are compromised, delays and "flutter" undermine the QOS and those attempting to communicate become unhappy.

DRILLDOWN

When it comes to acceptance and implementation of voice-over IP technology, the industry is entering its salad days and good things are only going to get better. That's the opinion given in a Cahners In-Stat Group report, which predicts that VOIP will become a $4 billion industry by 2003, an increase of some 280 percent from where the industry was in 1999 when the study was conducted.

Of course, this will require a few changes in the way the various industry segments view on-line telephony. Internet service providers (ISPs) will need to evolve into Internet telephony service providers (ITSPs) and the industry as a whole will have to move from the cost-per-minute rate into some other formula to retain its profitability as the market changes. The emergence of private intranets and extranets as the pipeline for this service also will aid in public acceptance and usage, not to mention growth of VOIP itself.

Fortunately, technology continues to step forward on what some still consider an immature technology, making VOIP one of the next big waves of the future.

How It All Works

No matter what your interest in voice-over IP, please remember there are two cardinal rules that govern implementation and access to the technology:

- Voice and data transmission needs are different. As such, each has certain system configuration requirements in order to be successfully sent and received. This is a reality rather than an option.
- Because voice and data transmission needs are different, your system will have to be reconfigured to accommodate the needs of both if you're going to run each through the Internet. This, too, isn't an option.

Understanding and adjusting to both of these rules will be critical to successful VOIP implementation, no matter what your company's size or complexity.

The PC-to-PC communication discussed earlier still lies at the conceptual heart of voice-over IP. But today's efforts have evolved into fully configured, gateway-based systems that tie a company's private branch exchange (PBX) or local area network (LAN) with calls coming in through the Internet. The goal of either is to convert voice transmissions from their packet-based environment to a circuit-switched domain. Usually this is done with a digital signal processor and involves preparing a voice sample for transmission through compression and removal of vocal jitter. That signal is then repacketed and sent out over the Internet to the appropriate receiver either through the PBX or LAN, across a T1 line and out the door.

This is a slightly different way of handling calls than those coming in over preexisting telephone lines and through the PBX without having to go through the voice-over IP gateway to be bagged, bundled and digitized. It will require a different technology configuration, perhaps, than what you have and/or are used to. At the very least, it means more work and higher costs up front. But long-term results could add up to significant savings.

Scalability is always an issue in any program migration, and it's no different for voice-over IP. While cost savings can be considerable, especially when multiples of hundreds or even thousands of users are involved, adjustment time and effort also can be a challenge. Smaller private or enterprise-wide networks might find the task easier and less costly, even though they may sacrifice management of some higher-end services, such as billing. Less complex alternatives such as sound cards inserted into servers, switches in place of PBXs and gateway services may offer satisfactory options.

The appropriate option also may be determined by the services you choose to bundle together. When GTE Corporation investigated VOIP several years ago, it considered creating the following service bundles:

- Standard telephone service, the bread and butter of most providers as well as the key need for most businesses;
- Fax services, which don't offer the same challenges as voice conversations because there is no real-time developmental interaction among fax senders and receivers as there is among two people attempting to have a conversation;
- Voice mail and other messaging services, like faxes, consist of stored data and don't require interactivity; and
- New access devices, such as wireless technologies, which present many of the same challenges, along with a few new ones.

Whether you are the bundler or the recipient, decisions involving these key services may help point you in the direction you need to go more effectively than many components in your telecommunications strategic plan.

One of the greatest challenges facing voice transmission, of course, has to do with changes in operational protocols and methodologies. By comparison, data transmission—during which a signal is sent to the Internet service provider, who completes the transaction once the sender's ID has been verified—appears almost ridiculously easy.

The change comes in the nature of the role the ISP has to play to transmit what has now become a much more complex data stream. Used to being end points, ISPs must now become service switching points (SSPs) in a public network environment. Much of this came about because, under the previous configuration, many ISPs couldn't support the necessary QOS standards. More and more of them are moving toward using a combination of gatekeeper and gateway units to support the necessary services, including call setup, packeting and routing functions.

The gateway has allowed interested ISPs to serve as an interface between the public switched telephone network (PSTN) and the IP network, and to support the necessary operational functions. The gatekeepers can effectively interpret which direction PSTN and Internet service digital network (ISDN) transmissions are headed and how they should be coded in order to get there. The gatekeeper fills the role, also keeping the appropriate address lists and delivery protocols at the ready.

Helpful as all this is, it may not be enough with the evolution of the intelligent network and the greater demands being brought about with local number portability needs, including database queries for ported subscribers. To that end, Internet telephony service providers (ITSPs) are going to need a seamless connection to signaling system 7 (SS7) links and the ability to manage the more complex intelligent network performance requirements.

What this all means is the higher the level of service required, the more complex the networks must be. Internet telephony undoubtedly will continue improving its service profile, which means providers will need to be that much more nimble in dealing with the new, more complex systems. It's necessary to keep the voice transmission quality high. And at this end of spectrum, transmission quality is what will win the day, or at least the market share.

A Question of Quality

As mentioned earlier, the biggest brouhaha over VOIP has to do with QOS. The quality-of-service quotient looms large because of the real-time access and conversational challenges that crop up during voice exchanges. No telecom company wants to gain a reputation as the one whose transmissions stumble and crack, even if it only refers to the operational segment that occurs over the still-maturing Internet link. Changes in the layered protocols that drive many systems hold some hope for this sometimes dismal scenario.

Without getting too deep into tech-speak—we'll save that for your software developer/vendors—changes have been made at layer 2 and layer 3 protocols that will enable many systems to respond in a more timely and quality-conscious fashion.

Layer 2 protocols allow information packets to be prioritized into as many as eight different levels. This enables the switches to determine delivery order and priorities for the information, thus slowing down the transmission glut and arranging it in an orderly, logical fashion. Addition of more infor-

LEARNING VOIP-SPEAK

Voice-over-Internet protocol has created its own set of special terms and acronyms. The following list will help you keep the words and their meanings straight:

- Call Leg—a connection between router and either end point in the telephony chain that travels over a bearer channel.

- Committed information rate (CIR)—the average rate of information transfer as part of a Frame Relay PVC as identified by the subscriber.

- Codec—a coding/decoding device that changes analog signals to a digital bit stream and vice versa through pulse code modulation.

- Dial peer—a call end point, either voice-over-Internet protocol (VOIP) or plain old telephone service (POTS).

- Dual-tone multifrequency (DTMF)—two voice-band tones used simultaneously.

- E&M—literally Ear & Mouth, figuratively recEive & transMit; a trunking arrangement used for both switch-to-switch and switch-to-network arrangements.

- FIFO—literally first in, first out; a buffering scheme in which data bits are retrieved in the order in which they are received, much like your calls are when you're put on hold.

- Foreign exchange office (FXO)—the interface that connects to the public switched telephone network (PSTN) office and is offered on a standard telephone.

- Foreign exchange station (FXS)—the interface connecting to your telephone that supplies the dial tone, ring and voltage.

- Multilink PPP—the point-to-point protocol that's responsible for splitting, recombining and sequencing data for transmission across links such as phone lines.

- PBX—a private branch exchange, which functions as a privately owned central switching office for routing calls, usually within an organization or company.

- POTS—the plain old telephone service refers to single-line accounts and is pretty much just like it sounds.

- PSTN —the public switched telephone network also is known as your local phone company.

- QOS—the quality of service is the level of service provided to subscribers; it is one of the most important considerations in voice-over IP.

- RSVP—resource reservation protocol supports all resources across the IP network.

mation to the IP headers at layer 3 enables the system to more easily spot what is, in essence, "priority mail" and make sure that's delivered first. Class-based queuing is the engine that drives this and is critical for helping decide how much bandwidth a message deserves, thus supporting a higher level of delivery quality.

Resource reservation protocol (RSVP) is the mechanism that puts all this into the hands of the service provider. Like the others, it's a critical part of the mix. In order to bring it all together, your quality policy must be available to all devices on your computer network. A common open policy service (COPS) applies standards of control to any network from end to end.

The bottom line: Your QOS must be managed aggressively if you want your VOIP to be successful. Despite the time we spend talking about hardware, software and connectivity, such a system is first and foremost about meeting and beating customer expectations. Any system you create must do this; otherwise, you'll soon find that you're in the wrong business.

Systems also require scalability for growth and allowance for the latency that inevitably occurs. Voice-over IP has a strong impact on the business-to-business market. That's where most of the early growth will occur. There will be precious little patience for those systems unable to perform to standard. QOS will be the new standard of the future, and if you have an interest in either end of Internet telephony, that's a boat you won't want to miss.

Chapter S9
Watch Your ASP!

The enormous growth in the power, influence and reach of computers, especially since the advent of the Internet and the burgeoning of on-line networks, has created tremendous opportunities for businesses and consumers alike. Along with those opportunities, however, come obligations, many of which have become both difficult and expensive to meet.

For mid-size to small companies, especially, the need to run with the big dogs has never been more compelling, in terms of both opportunities and rewards. At the same time, the cost of entering the race has become enormous. Those that want their bite to match their bark had better be ready to lay out the necessary expenses, or tuck their tails between their legs and run away home.

The probable solution for many firms? Leave data processing and management needs to alternative service providers, also known as ASPs. Positioned as separate computer and network service firms suitable for outsourcing all of the most basic data processing and management, ASPs can function as a permanent off-site operational solution for companies that can't or won't bear the cost or deal with the hassle of the ever-changing computer/network environment.

Sound good? Many companies think so and have moved their more mundane functions to an ASP for management. An equal number find ASPs' off-the-shelf cookie-cutter approach insufficient to handle highly specialized operations or necessarily customized software needs. A growing number, too, have raised concerns about data security, struggled with the outside management of proprietary information, or argued over contractual obligations, pricing and delivery with ASPs they formerly had regarded as partners in managing their processes. Many say that the old industry acronym WYSIWYG—What You See Is What You Get—doesn't necessarily apply when dealing with ASPs.

Perhaps, they say, the new acronym PYWANCAWYA—Proceed Ye With All Necessary Caution And Watch Your ASP—might be more appropriate.

Whatever your experience or concern, be advised that ASPs—at least some of them—are here to stay. A Gartner Group/Dataquest survey predicted the ASP market would increase more than tenfold, climbing from $2.7 billion in 1999 to $22.7 billion by 2003. At the same time, Gartner estimates the number of players will decrease by more than 60 percent and predicts that, by 2004, there may be as few as 20 alternative service firms fighting over what by then may have become a massive marketplace.

Watch your ASP, indeed, and make sure that what you invest your data processing needs in, while here today, will not be gone tomorrow.

A Little History and a Lot of Potential

ASPs are a fairly new phenomenon, even for the computer industry, bubbling to the surface in the late '90s, when market demand for service outpaced many companies' abilities to match the levels of sophistication necessary to compete effectively. The concept of shared services, however, goes back to when company mainframe or minicomputers participated in timeshare arrangements with central service providers to reduce costs and access expertise. Dialing in, often through dumb terminals, firms could capitalize on cooperative software systems that met their needs. Timeshare arrangements offered generic applications providing subscribers with basic business functions, eliminating their need to invest in the hardware, software and technical staff necessary to make it work. For those of you already familiar with ASP operations, does this sound at all familiar?

As company finances and sophistication grew, most firms graduated to their own enterprise resource planning systems, labeled ERPs, and customized software that met their own evolving needs. The fortunes of generic timeshare companies ebbed and flowed with the growth of the industry. Many disappeared, while others morphed into what are now called ASPs as the demands of increasingly sophisticated systems and a growing number of companies converged at a price range that exceeded the reach, or at least the desire, of those who needed services. ASP entrepreneurs saw a resurgence in need and have sought to fill it. It's a basic business principle and ASPs' relative success will depend on how well they manage what has become for others the most compelling, complex and expensive part of their operation.

But the new iteration brought its own value-added spin to the mix that went beyond cost and servicing issues. High-speed networking capabilities combined with increasingly powerful and inexpensive hardware capacity to create an IT environment increasingly more portable and flexible than those in the past have been. An increase in higher quality prepackaged software matched by a decrease in capable, available IT professionals made the market for generic solutions both attractive and accessible while addressing compelling technology and human resource issues simultaneously. Couple that with the rapidly-changing IT environment and increased accessibility through Internet channels and suddenly ASPs can make an offer most companies can't afford to refuse. And suddenly a whole new industry is born.

DRILLDOWN

ASPs offer chief technology officers one more avenue to get their jobs done, but it will be the CTO's job to determine how viable that avenue is for his or her particular company. Off-the-shelf software options may be fine for small or medium-size enterprises (SMEs), but may have no application whatsoever for the technologically complex Fortune 500 company.

Collaborative relationships, the types in which most ASPs specialize, will be the way of the future for IT, but questions about both security and access to proprietary data beyond the company's firewall may make ASPs a non-option for some. Web delivery will be common for most of us from this day forward, but who controls the internal post office, once again, is a matter for the CTO to decide. Outsourcing and quick fixes simply aren't for everyone.

By Definition and Architecture

Part of the problem with any label is that a wide variety of pretenders to the throne tend to gather in its shadow and vie for attention. ASPs are no different and have created no small confusion among companies struggling to understand not only what they are, but also what they can do. The challenges in some segments of the marketplace as well as misunderstood viability of their applications have only exacerbated this situation. A formal definition is in order.

By definition, an ASP is any organization that offers specific software-based business services or solutions on a subscription or fee-for-use basis that are deliverable via the Internet or other networked arrangement. The definition is succinct, complete, and to the point and focuses on the delivery mechanism. In the days of the old timeshare arrangements, of course, there was no Internet. Like so many other things, the Internet has made the growth and proliferation of ASPs both possible and profitable.

Functionally speaking, ASPs operate a little like leasing agencies. Companies gain computer applications and functionality, often at a level that outstrips their existing capabilities and enhances their services well beyond any reasonable expectation. They do this literally by renting time and, through access, professional applications and services from the ASP without investing in their own ERPs, technical staff, and proprietary software development. Moreover, subscription-based payments allow the company to pay for only the services it uses, freeing up capital for use in other areas of company development.

From a delivery standpoint, the ASP itself is structurally simple. Most serve simply as hosts for Web-enabled applications accessible and scalable to the client companies. Mix in some security software to validate paying users and maybe a virtual private network to prevent data leakage to the Web and you have your basic ASP setup.

Of course, most ASPs employ something a little more complex—although not much more—and must adjust for the scale of business that they eventually end up serving. Most ASPs take a four-tier approach to their operations:

- An initial data layer stores and handles information relevant to its hosted applications. This is most often held in a relational database to promote easier access.

- A second applications layer serves as home to the operations and application-based logic that drives the programs and facilitates the client relationship.

- A third layer is devoted to Web service and provides the necessary muscle to make sure the data and applications are delivered through the Web to subscribers.

- The Web server layer delivers data directly to the user interface layer, more familiarly known as a browser, that enables subscriber access through standard Web protocols such as http or HTML.

Such seeming ease of operation, however, is complicated by the number of users ASPs host. To host and serve thousands of subscribers requires the ASP to operate from a data center that supports the four-tier operation. The ASP may have either one data center or a series of them, the latter designed to reduce the distance between subscribers and the system. In either case, the center(s) must be geared for 24/7 operations, with the necessary redundancy to protect against unexpected system failure and downtime along with the appropriate technical support. In either case, too, communications management between subscribers and the ASP requires some pretty big pipes. That usually means bundles of the necessary T3 lines to keep the center(s) functional and in service around the clock.

The description once again makes the point that, technically speaking, there is nothing new or innovative about ASP architecture. Their structure and function hearken back to the old timesharing days, which are as old as the first PC itself. What's different is the value-enhanced business model under which such systems operate. It's that model that's the source of the opportunities, as well as some of the trials and tribulations ASPs are causing today. We'll discuss each of those in turn.

DRILLDOWN

Growth is good for an industry, but the introduction of ASPs has changed the way independent software vendors (ISVs) will do business from now on. In the earliest days, software developers created custom programs, capturing many clients for life—or at least for as long as it took them to muster the courage and financial acumen to switch to someone else's platform.

Through their partnership arrangements, ASPs offer companies greater flexibility and portability in getting their needs met, rendering almost moot the monopoly that ISVs had, at least with existing clients. Now ISVs themselves have morphed into ASPs, with mixed results. Do they maintain allegiance to their own lines in hopes of capturing income and market share for their own products? Or do they promote flexibility and variety of choice in an effort to hang onto increasingly savvy customers who know that application, not brand name, will help them accomplish their own strategic goals?

Given the predicted fallout of ASPs in the years to come, that's a tough choice, but one on which ISVs' future may depend.

More Confusion

Understanding basic ASP architecture is just the beginning of playing the getting-to-know-you game with this particular industry segment. Not all ASPs are created equal and, more to the point, only some exist as freestanding, full-service agencies capable of meeting all subscribers' needs. Some ASPs entered the world as independents; others have been born of larger service providers in an attempt to capture share in this particular market. Still others are an amalgam of partner providers and serve as a clearinghouse for connection to the necessary specialties. In most cases, it's very much like comparing apples to oranges. And bananas. And watermelons.

Industry watchers have identified several different specific types of ASPs. Currently, the industry is characterized by three basic avenues to ASP service:

- "Pure-play" ASPs are companies formed especially to serve as ASPs, integrating product and service components from other companies and sources. Some do develop and offer their own solutions, but most serve as host to third-party solutions, offering subscribers support through their data centers and connectivity through partnerships to primary software providers that meet their needs.

- Internet service providers (ISPs), originally designed to host Web sites, provide the type of data center infrastructure and communications networks on which ASPs are built. In addition to function and connectivity, ISPs also offer a higher level of computer horsepower, security and disaster recovery software, as well as more storage capacity than a lot of other providers.

- Independent software vendors (ISVs) also function as ASPs, but their goal is often to promote, utilize and ultimately sell their own software. That may be a perfectly acceptable alternative if they have what the subscriber wants, or it might be seen as limiting in terms of the options and arrangements that could be made if a wider choice through an independent agency were able to be arranged.

No matter which route a company chooses to go, however, it's important to realize that a variety of providers play one role or another in supporting ASP operations. All ASP foundations are based on computer platforms that offer scalable services to support large numbers of simultaneous users. Most of these platform providers, such as Sun Microsystems and Hewlett-Packard, welcome this new role and see this as an opportunity to increase market share. There's nothing wrong with that, especially if the services they provide support the ASP and adequately meet subscriber needs.

Independent software vendors, already mentioned above, play a role no matter what the configuration. In turnkey situations, they may be the partners to which the pure-play ASPs or ISPs turn for services. It's the software, after all, that drives the applications. Often they're at the heart of the function, and no more so than when they themselves are the ASPs.

The new systems also rely to some degree on ASP aggregators, such as Jamcracker, to integrate and bundle services and delivery methodologies for end users. Aggregators offer services from platforms often driven by single browsers, allowing subscriber businesses access to any number of tools, resources and/or information.

Portal applications and service providers also play a role in helping identify, sort and deliver the right information without a lot of chaff. In fact, service provider AT&T developed its Ecosystem for ASPs to provide the necessary backbone, colocation, data center and network services to subscriber companies. The portals, in turn, sort the data and deliver what the subscriber needs and wants.

There's even a role for independent service providers, such as accounting/consulting firms Ernst & Young and Deloitte & Touche, to advise businesses and assist companies with ASP and Web service integration. Such agency services go well beyond technical support to include strategic and management consulting, business analysis, systems training and other support to help companies make the right ASP decisions.

Clearly, an ASP's role as service aggregator is critical to the growth and development of the services provided. Whether it will be the pure-play ASPs, the ISPs, or the software vendors who rise to the top in the coming shakeout, however, is anyone's guess. There are, however, key functions that surviving ASPs will need to master in order to stay on top of the service curve. These functions include the following:

- Effective network operations and management will be critical as subscribers look for uninterrupted support from their ASP, and client network problems can't stand in the way of whatever the ASP promised in its service agreement.

- Adequate data facilities with scalable growth potential are important, especially in terms of technologically advanced storage facilities.

- High-performance middleware and other application strategies should be flexible and adaptable to client needs. The supporting maintenance also must make the grade.

- Access to transport methodologies, especially from multiple platforms, will prove a real asset not only to clients but also to the ASP itself. This is one area that clients usually can't afford to support themselves.

- Finally, an emphasis on integration—and that includes systems as well as business integration—will offer the expertise and flexibility that could give ASPs the leading edge when it comes to service.

Admittedly, this is an expansive and potentially expensive supply chain to maintain. Running an ASP is not an easy task. In order to make it an economical one, however, the right pieces need to be in place. Otherwise an ASP shouldn't bank on surviving the coming shakeout.

Deficits and Benefits

Locking into a relationship with an ASP is a business decision of the first magnitude. The right relationship can make your business, but the wrong one may cripple, if not kill it outright. ASPs aren't right for everyone in every situation, but they may be more right for you than you may think. It all depends on understanding the pros and cons of the process. Here are some to consider.

I Want My ASP Because:

- ASP support gives me freedom from increasingly complex, costly and ever-changing IT management details and parameters. Without those headaches, I can concentrate on my company's core competencies while knowing that critical IT tasks are being handled competently, professionally and well beyond the degree to which I could do it myself.

- More options and more effective implementation are the hallmarks of today's ASPs. My company's basic tasks get handled, but I get more in terms of value-added services and advanced capabilities than I even knew to ask for. This includes easier, faster access to improvements in programs and functionality. With my ASP, the whole is significantly greater than the sum of its parts.

- When I compare my monthly subscription fees to the cost of ownership, maintenance and staffing my own ERP, the ASP's economies of scale offer me a cheaper alternative. Industry has shown that I can cut my costs by 30 percent to 50 percent, freeing up critical capital for other, more important uses.

- And when all is said and done, the decreased implementation on my part, coupled with the high-level support I receive from ASP technical staff, gives me greater expertise at a lower prices than I would have if I tried to do it all myself.

I Don't Want My ASP Because:

- There's no guarantee my ASP will be around after the shakeout. Besides, wildfire growth is usually followed by a steep decline and I don't know how stable my ASP is financially or operationally.

- For the most part, the ASP model still hasn't proved itself in the long term. There may be long-range problems that have yet to show their faces. There also may be cracks developing in quality of service issues so critical to my company's success.

- Loss of control and lack of security may be issues for me now, or in the future. Once my ASP has my data, there's no telling what it may do in terms of holding my business hostage. Since much of that data is sensitive and proprietary, my inability to exercise my own rigorous controls over its use and dissemination quite frankly makes me nervous.

- My biggest concern has to do with my limited ability to customize processes and software beyond off-the-shelf alternatives so that I can grow applications with my growing company. The inability to do that could cost me my competitive edge in the marketplace and, eventually, market share.

Granted, these concerns can all be addressed by high-level, capably run ASPs, but no firm should go into any relationship without understanding the potential pitfalls in the road to progress.

Mastering Your Fate

Whether you do or do not choose to align your services with an ASP will depend less on their capabilities and presence in the marketplace and more on how they fit within your own strategy. Too many firms turn their backs on the fact that ASP applicability goes only as far as their own corporate strategies allow. The approach may be a desirable alternative, or it may have no role to play whatsoever. But that needs to be the choice of the CTO or executive team at the potential subscriber company, not merely the desire of the ASP to hitch its wagon to your star. Logical as that seems, there's always someone who forgets this is a strategic decision as well as an operational consideration.

When it comes down to it, two key factors lie at the heart of an ASP decision:

- Given the set of the firm's functional requirements, how unique do the IT alternatives need to be? Basic business functions, such as accounts payable and payroll, are identical from company to company, making them likely operations that can be off-loaded onto an external provider. Custom-driven functions unique to the company or its products, on the other hand, will fare poorly in the generic systems world of ASPs. Given the balance between the two, what is the likelihood of a successful ASP relationship?

- How critical is tight control over the IT support operations? One of the big fears in dealing with any ASP is potential security breaches and accessibility to proprietary information. When the data and/or operations do not reside within the company's firewall, then the likelihood of potential leakage is greater than if they did. In addition, the ability to make quick changes as well as access to company experts is delayed at least by one step. What a company may save in cost may be sacrificed in quick access and safety.

In terms of a generic answer to those issues, it would seem that operations in which economies of scale make ASPs a suitable economic alternative are likely candidates for transfer. Add to that the need for simplicity of operations and reduced customization and you may find that ASPs offer a viable strategic alternative for the mission and goals of your company.

The smart CTO also will take one step back to make sure that what's been done as a customized function now might not be better or more cheaply handled generically, an advantage an ASP could provide. A lot of legacy software evolved through the creation of unique alternatives to common everyday business operations. If you haven't yet jettisoned those old systems and ways of operation, then an ASP may be a likely way to do it. If that matches your corporate strategy, then that may be a good step to take.

There are other advantages to choosing an ASP to manage your operations, no matter what the size of your firm:

- ASPs offer access to what might be unaffordable functionality or new tools that your company hasn't yet accessed. Remember that, for many ASPs, the whole is greater than the sum of the parts. Cost savings are one thing, but enhanced functionality can not only address needs on the expense side of your operation, but also provide new opportunities to enhance revenue. A more holistic view is critical to making the right decision.
- ASPs can offer rapid scalability to companies that need to grow but don't quite have the necessary horsepower to do so. Again, this is an expense versus revenue opportunity equation. An ASP can help control growth cost and negate investments in unnecessary overhead, while still providing the same level of opportunity to test the waters and sail new seas of commerce.

- And speaking of commerce, don't forget the ASPs' key contribution to your enterprise—to reduce the need and resulting cost of in-house expertise and to support the conservation of capital and its redirection into other, more critical uses. As an outsourced IT department, an ASP may be able to do all the things you need done at a lower price. If that meets your needs without posing any undue threats, allowing you to concentrate on your core competencies, then an ASP may be the alternative for you.

If making the jump to an ASP makes sense to you, your own organizational priorities and goals should drive selection. Functionality, reliability, adaptability and scalability all factor in the equation. Whether you choose a pure-play ASP, an expanded ISV or a multitiered ISP depends on the nature, age and size of your enterprise. Pure-play models may be a better match for start-ups and smaller enterprises that need the flexibility and scalability. Established enterprises with high data storage needs can take advantage of an ISP's capabilities. And if you're already deeply involved in a specific software platform, accessing that provider's ASP capabilities makes a great deal of sense. The deciding factor in all cases, of course, will be determined by the scope and needs of your own organization.

DRILLDOWN

The big advantages ASPs offer is hot new services, the hottest of which may be managing business intelligence. By taking company data, cleansing and sorting it, the ASP has a wealth of raw materials with which to work. It also does the difficult task of housecleaning, but by preselected information type rather than by mere intellectual file tossing.

Once the data is pure, then business analytical tools are put in place and made available to company executives, who then can sift and winnow in ways meaningful to the individual, the company and its mission. Turning data into information allows for better decision making and more value to the company.

But you get what you pay for, and good business intelligence systems aren't cheap. Expect to pay a monthly subscription fee of between $10,000 and $150,000, depending on the size, complexity and depth of the data in question. Whether this is an expense or an investment will depend on how well company executives are able to use the information. Sharing the data and paying the fee is just the beginning.

Before jumping to light speed, however, make sure you analyze all potential vendors based not on claims but on past performance and positive references. Different vendors specialize in different industries and you need one especially attuned to yours.

Moreover, while working with a start-up ASP would be a kind thing to do, only past performance will tell you what their levels of reliability and performance have been and likely will be for you. Vendors unable or unwilling to match your service needs with their capabilities, and to be flexible enough to address your needs and commit to your timetables rather than theirs will not be a good match. As for price, remember that value, not cost, should determine the relationship.

Deeper Analyses

Functionality, flexibility and price are the key drivers in choosing an ASP. That goes without saying. But too few companies consider the nature of the ASP as a business itself when it comes to choosing their future IT partner. Knowing whether the ASP will be there tomorrow is as critical as knowing that they do what you need them to do today. Care should be taken when it comes to performing due diligence on the business as a business.

One of the most critical factors driving this is what was mentioned earlier. Researchers predict that by 2004 the market will be in the hands of as few as 20 ASPs. That could mean tremendous business falloff in a very short period of time. Backing the right horse will mean clearly understanding the following business components:

- Is the ASP profitable? IT is still very much a go-go environment and if the firm isn't showing a positive bottom line, that's not only bad for its own business, but it also means it probably won't be around very long, which is potentially bad for your business.
- Does the ASP have enough experience with its own outsourcing and partnering relationships to guarantee that it will be able to keep pace with industry progress? No ASP is an island, entire of itself. Those that say they are will soon sink out of sight or leave the business altogether.

- What type of delivery track record does the ASP have? If it can't show you progress in client service, then perhaps it hasn't made enough that's worth mentioning. That's a red flag if ever there was one.

- Finally, and perhaps most importantly, how effective is the ASP as an integrator/aggregator of services? Remember that whether pure-play, ISP or ISV, connectivity to other vendors is to a greater or lesser degree the driving strength behind an ASP. It's also where the greatest level of service falls off. Those that can't control or at least guarantee certain service levels from their own partners will cost you time and money and cause you headaches. Remember, forewarned is forearmed when it comes to understanding this key strength.

The idea of controlling vendors is the place where most ASP relationships fracture, and failure to live up to service level agreements (SLAs) is the breaking point for many relationships. If the ASP has no SLAs with its own vendors, the likelihood of being able to live up to yours is remote. That the Gartner Group predicts a failure rate of 85 percent of ASPs in this area does not bode well for the growth and development of the industry overall. The best a company can do is make sure the SLA is specific in its demands and articulates punitive measures for failing to meet those demands. Just like any general contractor, the ASP should be responsible for failures on the part of its subcontractors. An ASP unable or unwilling to accept this responsibility may best be left alone.

Quality of service issues may be accredited to failure in bandwidth capacity or a host of technical issues. Scalability to meet upticks in demand, along with the appropriate network infrastructure, are part and parcel of any agreement you strike with an ASP. That is, after all, the reason you engaged their services in the first place and should be part of the hefty fee you're paying to them. Do not assume, however, that such caveats don't exist unless they're clearly covered in the SLA.

Speaking of pricing, negotiating the type of fee, along with the amount, will be vital to a good working relationship as well as to the continued fiscal well-being of your firm. In general, the ASP industry supports three types of fee arrangements:

- The flat monthly fee usually covers a basic package of services as negotiated during your contractual phase. Additional services may be available for an additional fee based on capacity, or a company may be able to trade up to a higher level of service for a greater cost.

- Per-user costs are determined by the number of people accessing the ASP from a single company along with the level of service they access. Generally, the higher the number of users, the lower the per-user cost. This seems most appropriate for back-office users with specific needs and high volume.
- Transaction-based pricing comes into play primarily in e-commerce and can be used to manage ebb and flow of seasonal businesses. Fees rise right along with sales, which can pose a problem for an ASP during slow business months for the client company. Because of this, transaction-based pricing tends to be more costly than other types that produce more reliable income streams.

Once again, price is an important factor in your decision. The type of payment plan chosen should be based on the strategic and operational needs of the client company, rather than the preference of the ASP.

Drafting a Contract

Given all the caveats, it would seem that entering into a contractual agreement with an ASP would be a little bit like making a deal with the devil. Needless to say, it's not that bad. But exercise all due caution and remember that there are a few things to look for. Otherwise, you may have a hell of a time getting the services you want and need.

- An ASP contract consists of three parts: the contract itself, a statement of work (SOW) and the service level agreement (SLA). These can be three separate documents or one longer document with three distinct parts. The differences among all three are equally as distinct. The SOW tells you exactly the type of services for which you've contracted, while the SLA articulates acceptable levels of service within this work scenario. The contract forms the legally binding glue between documents and outlines prices, penalties and procedures associated with the legal consummation of the SOW and SLA.
- Both the SOW and SLA should be complete in their service expectations and explain fully what will happen when those expectations aren't met. More relationships have been undone by inadequate detail than by anything else. Both of these need to describe what's going to happen and what will occur if it doesn't happen as fully as humanly possible.

DRILLDOWN

One of the most intriguing and still relatively unexplored ASP application sets has been their relationships to home offices. While small- to medium-size enterprises often receive greater benefits from ASPs, it's this smallest of the small—home offices—that can stand to profit from advanced protocols and increased capabilities without making major hardware or software investments themselves. As always, however, cautions apply.

Unlike the service firms of the past, an ASP's greatest strengths are found in its portabilities. That's thanks to its Web-based delivery mechanisms and browser-driven operations. For the home officer or single-person entrepreneur, access to business tools and increased bandwidth can make an ASP an amazingly sweet proposition.

By renting disk space on the provider's system, you can access your files from any PC with browser and modem capabilities. That means you don't have to lug your laptop to appointments as long as cyber café capabilities are available. You can access the ASP's system for e-mail, calendar capabilities and file storage. Many also offer you access to generic business forms and other office services at what appears to be a bargain-basement price compared to supporting your own brick-and-mortar facility.

Some ASPs also will host your Web page, giving you complete access to a suite of services and offering virtual desktop capabilities, allowing you to do your work anywhere you can log on in the known universe. By accessing the ASP's increased bandwidth, you can communicate faster and jump farther than you otherwise might be able to through your own ISP.

On the downside, you'll need a DSL modem if you expect to communicate in anything resembling real time. Know, too, that you are one small potato in an ever-growing field and far from being the pick of the current customer crop.

In the worst case, your ASP could disappear overnight—a big shakeout is predicted in the next 18 months—and you would be the last to know. But if the cons don't outweigh the pros, the leap to an ASP could be your next and best business move.

- Make sure there are exit strategies and clauses that fit the need of your business. Sometimes things just don't work out, and you'll need avenues for exiting without damaging your company, its operations or its reputation. Pay special attention to process and data ownership when drafting your exit clause. Make sure you have leeway to switch suppliers within the ASP if need be or to exit from the ASP entirely if the need becomes great enough.

ASPs won't be leaving the scene any time soon. In point of fact, depending on the development of the industry, they may become permanent gateways to the Internet, aggregators of services for an increasingly complex computerized world, preferred providers of critical software components, or all of the above. Even now, when it comes to services, it's a case of ASP and ye shall receive, at least in most cases.

Knowing what to ask your ASP and knowing what you can expect to receive goes a long way to getting the satisfaction you need.

Chapter S10
Untangling the Supply Chain

As a dot.com merchant, or even if you run a standard business operation with Web site activity, you know that making the sale is the lion's share of the effort you need to support commerce. You've developed the right product, identified the critical market, mounted the most effective marketing and advertising you could think of and sent your strongest sales message into the consumer stratosphere in hopes of hooking a live one. Or 1,000.

Now that you've done it, the rest is easy, right? You process the credit card number and, upon acceptance, ship the product or direct the service toward the customer. Sale completed, buyer satisfied, commerce achieved, yes?

If only life were that easy. Consider the following scenario:

As a fledgling dot.com, you're pleased to the point of being overwhelmed when your new site is inundated with hits and overrun with customers. You thought you'd uncovered a corner of the flabberjabber market that hadn't yet been exploited, and you were right. Orders from consumers and resellers are coming in hand over fist. With research and development bills to pay and salaries beginning to mount up, you couldn't be happier.

You quickly begin processing orders, banking income and contacting your suppliers about getting their butts in gear and shipping the supplies and subassemblies you need for final product assembly at your shop that will satisfy the orders you've received. But you come to find out that what works well in theory doesn't quite happen in practice.

Several of the suppliers operate through a much more antiquated system and they themselves need time to get the raw materials from their suppliers. In some cases, they don't have the necessary inventory on hand

and, in one case, they can't even get the missing piece, forcing redesign and last-minute substitutions two rungs down the ladder. You have no choice but to sit and wait until they get their ducks in a row before you can hope to meet the orders, the money from which you've already collected, banked and, in some cases, spent satisfying your own expenses.

Well, things couldn't get worse, could they? Think again. The flabberjabber component you've perfected is seasonal in appeal. Your window of opportunity is closing and it will take another 12 full months to generate interest again. Your suppliers' missed deadlines mean that you, too, miss meeting your promised ship dates. That makes your customers very unhappy, so much so that many of them cancel their orders. Those that don't watch the season come and go with only token shipments being received. By the time others in your supply chain have figured things out, your market has dried up and blown away.

Wait, this gets worse. In the interim your company, which has gone public, has created quite a splash with the product that it has uncorked. Wall Street paid a lot of attention and enthusiastic investors of all sorts have purchased a lot of your firm's stock, hoping for the big payoff at the end of the season. Now that word has reached them of the kinks in your supply chain, the investment feeding frenzy of a few months ago has shifted into reverse and they're turning and running from your stock just like it was Black Monday all over again. Share value plummets and market commentators have already predicted your demise. That lovely little warehouse of product you have finally managed to amass will sit idle until next year at this time, long after Chapter 11 protection has become the focal point of your new strategic plan.

Admittedly, that bleak scenario contains the worst of all possible worlds. But none of that is out of the question for firms of any size that haven't taken care to make sure that all rungs in the ladder are solid and lead to that ultimate goal of making the sale and satisfying the customer. The following scenario shows how it might have happened had the right cautions been put in place:

Your position in the flabberjabber market couldn't be better. Your new proprietary application satisfies a long-stated need and customers are clamoring for your product. You stand to make a bundle if you can capture the attention of your own suppliers and get them to step to your tune and meet your needs rather than simply addressing theirs. Do that and you'll be guaranteed a happy and financially healthy future in the business.

Fortunately for you, your sense of strategic development played into your original planning. You made sure that everyone with whom you planned to deal was on-line and up to speed in terms of just-in-time inventory management and fulfillment. In fact, the one company with whom you wanted to deal that wasn't Web-savvy was sent back for a crash course in supply-chain management. Come back in six months and show us what you can do and we'll talk, you told them, raising the bar against their past performance.

The season is upon you and the orders pour in. Your staff is busy over two shifts, putting subassemblies received from suppliers through the finishing touches and shipping finished product out to willing customers and resellers eager to capitalize on your market niche. Rolling warehouses—semi-trucks, really, uplinked via satellite to their main offices—know when and where to deliver materials, supplies and subassemblies to skilled workers in your various plants. You challenge suppliers as well as staff, rewarding the ones who work the fastest and most efficiently with perks, premiums and, most important of all, increased business. You begin to fulfill your orders in record time, meeting and beating your promised delivery dates.

Wall Street, having already sat up and taken notice when your new niche filler was announced, is delighted by your performance. Buyers are clamoring to become involved and your stock value soars. You're trading at a premium rate and brokers, buyers and especially your stockholders and board couldn't be happier. By the end of the season you have posted record profits, seized significant market share and been featured on the cover of your own trade industry publication, not to mention success stories in ancillary business publications about "the genius in the process" and "the guru of supply-chain management."

When it comes right down to it, it simply doesn't get any better than this. Until next year, that is.

A fairy tale in the making? An ugly duckling story gone good? Perhaps, but there are more and more firms every day discovering that their fortunes can be made or lost based on how effectively the links in their supply chain are interacting. Slipped linkages can mean lost business and lost business can mean lost enterprise. English poet George Herbert knew what he was talking about when he penned the following:

> For want of a nail, the shoe is lost.
> For want of a shoe, the horse is lost.
> For want of a horse, the rider is lost.
> For want of a rider, the battle is lost.

That same methodology works in business, too, especially on the supply-chain management side. Ask any dot.com now under Chapter 11 protection and they'll tell you.

DRILLDOWN

Supply-chain management is the flow of merchandise from the manufacturer through the distributor/warehouse and on to the ultimate consumer. The faster that merchandise moves through the supply chain, the less costly it is for the seller and the more profitable that firm becomes. Handling and storage expenses are pared and revenue is more quickly realized. That's really all there is to the equation; however, getting there from here often is a challenge.

Some distributors have found that bar coding works as well at the distribution center as it does at the ultimate point of sale. Operationally, bar coding facilitates the transfer of information, in this case production identification, automatically and with the least amount of time and input. In the above equation that translates to expenses saved and revenue earned. And that's the focal point of the issue.

The Crux of It All

It's no secret that e-commerce has raised the stakes on marketing and sales worldwide. Customers are Web-savvy enough to know that, if you order a widget on-line, that order is immediately streamed into the fulfillment process at HQ. It shouldn't be a matter of days, but a matter of minutes—maybe even seconds—before your credit card has been charged and someone somewhere has put your purchase into a box or wrapped it in brown paper, affixed a mailing label with your name on it and thrown the thing on a conveyor belt to be loaded and trucked to the commercial carrier of choice for delivery.

In these days of increased Web commerce, sales happen that quickly. Fulfillment, on the other hand, is another story entirely. If there is an Achilles' heel to the process, it's the fact that merchandise doesn't move as fast or as freely as information. And there's no guarantee that companies that have mastered distribution of the latter have any expertise whatsoever with the former. In fact, what has caused some e-tailers to collapse like houses of cards has nothing to do with their technical savvy or on-line presence. It has everything to do with the follow-through or lack thereof. Now that we have the order, what do we do with it? It appears that not all players in this growing marketplace have thought through the answer completely.

If this were the only problem plaguing virtual companies, the challenge would be bad enough. But standard retailers who have become e-tailers from a defensive position are beginning to catch up, thanks to this very issue. Those that have been peddling product behind actual brick-and-mortar for generations understand the fulfillment challenge and are coming to this battle armed and dangerous to the dot.coms. They already know the hard part and are now putting the purely on-line competitors through a trial by fire that already has begun to sort out the ultimate industry survivors.

DRILLDOWN

Electronic supply-chain management also extends to such mundane issues as workplace management. Two trends have emerged that are bound to make it less mundane.

First, companies will see a switch from routine electronic purchasing to a more strategic approach, de-emphasizing simple savings on the cost of office supplies and taking things to a higher level on which companies ultimately can build portions of their operational budget. This will be critical to the increase in value for in-office supply-chain management.

Second, look for companies and their vendors to go beyond that relationship, forming alliances that move from meeting supply demands to market and product development. A company requiring special treatment or a customized product can meets its own need as well as increase its revenue by turning appropriate facets of its operations into new products and services. Such an emphasis could lead to skirmishes over who controls the supply chain, but in the end it will be the successful partnerships, not merely the strongest of the players, that come out ahead in this situation.

Companies are discovering fast that order fulfillment can be the most expensive component in making a sale. Someone once calculated that Amazon.com used to spend $40 to fulfill a $20 book order. Whether there is any truth to this old e-marketer's tale is unknown. The point of the matter is that failure to understand what's involved, as well as the proper way to go about fulfillment, can cripple or kill a business. It boils down to supply-chain management, in both product development and delivery. Without effective ways of reaching fulfillment—at any step in the process—no e-tailer can hope to survive. That means making better use of information, leveraging resources and mastering logistics are critical to making things happen the right way.

Mastering Fulfillment Concepts

Industry experts see electronic supply-chain management revolving around two core concepts. The first concept involves making greater use of information flows rather than the flow of physical goods. The second is to use existing technologies as much as possible to control and stage the last stretch of delivery of those goods to the customer. Although the two are different, they both share one facet in common. They both describe ways of minimizing the time, effort and cost of physically delivering goods to customers as a way to increase efficiency and involve the customer in the fulfillment of his or her purchase.

Different strategies exist and we'll discuss each in turn. But let's look at a shorthand example of each to get started.

We said information travels faster than physical goods. That means the ultimate delivery length needs to be minimized in order to improve efficiency and cut costs. The central warehouse in Passaic, NJ, while suitable for meeting the needs of customers in the tri-state area, is not an efficient or cost-effective alternative for delivery of goods to Chicago, Denver or Los Angeles. Regional delivery hubs connected by telephone, e-mail, and other electronic means that route information rather than crates, cases and containers are a better option.

But let's take that one step further. Denver is still a long way from Las Cruces, NM, and Kalispel, MT. A delivery option that further reduces those distances—say a semi-trailer truck outfitted with the necessary gear that can receive satellite transmissions or perhaps e-mail or Web orders to its on-board computer—is even better. The vehicle can serve as a rolling warehouse capable of changing direction and putting goods in the hands of the customers sometimes as soon as the same day of order. At this point that may be the ultimate in sending information rather than goods over the longest distances for greater result.

The most common example of goods delivery that involves customer participation on the last leg of the journey is the self-serve gas station. Some of us are still old enough to remember when filling up your car meant a team of pump jockeys filling the tank, checking the oil and washing the windows, all for 29.9 cents per gallon. For the last two decades we've done all that ourselves, and the price of gas has soared. Granted, this is not a high-tech example, but the point is clear. Once you discover the degree to which the customer is willing to participate in the delivery of the services for which he or she is paying, then you can improve the costs associated with delivery by engaging that involvement and sitting back to reap the benefits.

The good news here is that companies may not need to reinvent existing fulfillment systems to capitalize on supply-chain management in either concept or practice. Some audience segments may be satisfied with the fulfillment procedures the firm already has in place. Streamlined processes will help satisfy others while new techniques can be used to reach the most important market segments.

In some cases, fulfillment also can be outsourced, or the firm can participate in trading exchanges, cooperatives that support and provide fulfillment service for specific industries. Like businesses can partner to aid each other in capitalizing on delivery and other resources. Cargofinder, for example, is a firm

DRILLDOWN

If there is a single key to success in this area, it's the synchronization of all partners within the supply chain. Thanks to the need for lower inventories, higher revenues from a greater number of satisfied customers and reduced operating costs, experts estimate the return on investment could be realized in as little as three months depending on up-front costs and duration of synchronized efforts. Increased efficiencies also can lead to improved performance. Synchronization has helped Dell Computer gain the ability to process custom orders in as little as 36 hours. A high level of collaboration among supply-chain partners is the reason.

that locates empty space on cargo ships for companies looking to place shipments. The effort helps shippers take advantage of opportunities available that ultimately reduce the steps and/or time in the delivery side of the supply chain.

The ultimate step, of course, is tailoring delivery needs to the customer. Once again, this will involve the transmission of information first, followed by the shipment of physical goods second. Third-party involvement, such as through a trading exchange or other external consultants and service providers, may be the best way to meet this growing need.

E-fulfillment Strategies

E-commerce is an unforgiving mistress and it takes some innovative thinking and, occasionally, creative practices to make e-fulfillment successful. Finding the right strategy for your company is no easy task. Here are some starting points for you to ponder. All support the concepts mentioned above.

Logistics postponement.   We've said it before and we'll say it again: The transfer of information first, before the movement of physical goods is crucial when that information can positively affect the cost and the time involved in that transfer. The right information means products won't be shipped early, late, in error or inaccurately. Moreover, that information can be used strategically rather than merely informationally, so that innovative approaches to materials handling, packaging and shipping can be applied to fulfillment challenges.

We've previously mentioned the idea of the rolling warehouse, a semi filled with products and/or materials that communicates remotely with dispatch and delivers only the materials required in the most timely manner possible. Another similar strategy would be merge-in-transit, wherein shipment components from varying points of departure would meet during the transit process, saving time and cost compared to orders originating from some central distribution location. Computer shippers like Hewlett-Packard and Compaq use this technique to deliver computer components warehoused at various locations to a single destination.

Resource pooling.   Cooperation has become the key to competitive success and nowhere is this more evident than in the idea of resource pooling—sharing resources and product and distribution channels to satisfy customer needs. If the distance is too great, the material in question too bulky or heavy or some other logistical challenge impedes delivery time or cost, resource pooling can provide alternatives that, while not always ideal for the seller, make a lot more sense when it comes to satisfying the buyer.

Major airlines follow their own versions of resource pooling. If you've ever been bumped from one airline to another due to weather or mechanical considerations, you've been part of a resource pooling solution. Instead of leaving you high and dry, the airline would rather lose revenue from a flight segment to another carrier than lose you as a customer altogether. No one, including the new airline, is especially happy about this strategy, but it's better than the alternative, which is no strategy—and no flight for you—at all.

Improving delivery value density.   Shipping too little to too wide an area results in inefficiencies in economies of scale. Leveraging shipment to improve delivery value density improves the cost of fulfillment right along with the time involved.

The idea that information travels faster and cheaper than physical goods is connected to innovative regional distribution methodologies. By balancing the components within the equation, an e-tailer maximizes delivery while minimizing cost. Amazon.com would be hard-pressed to schedule delivery of books, CDs and other products using an Amazon.com fleet of delivery trucks, despite the fact that it would give them maximum control. The products are too small and the market too diverse for that. In this case, commercial carriers like the U.S. Postal Service offer a good balance of cost and service with minimal risk compared to the results ratio realized.

MacWarehouse takes this scenario one step further, turning its delivery methodology into a strategic advantage by insisting on using private sector commercial carriers at a negotiated discount rate. In addition to improving delivery times, a factor that everyone appreciates, the private sector carrier also offers services that are both traceable and insurable. That's critical for the type of products—computers, peripherals and software—that the company sells and ships.

By positioning the service as a delivery advantage and involving the consumer through a slightly higher shipping payment, MacWarehouse manages to satisfy both its need as well as its customers' desires for improved services and safer delivery.

That customer cooperation comes to fruition in *click-and-mortar* businesses (CAMs), designed to once again capitalize on consumer reach. In their full-blown form, CAMs really introduce consumers to the front end of the process through on-line technology that enables them to e-shop first, then go to the point of delivery to pick up their purchases.

Increasingly, car manufacturers are turning to that approach. Through research and reading the customer has a sense of what he or she wants in an automotive product, then goes to the manufacturer's Web site to research make, model and options available. There's even list price information, allowing the consumer to begin negotiations in his or her own mind and prepare for the sales discussion that inevitably lies ahead. Once the consumer has designed the ideal version of the desired vehicle, the Web site will help locate the closest match to the consumer's preferred pickup location.

CAMs operate in conjunction with brick-and-mortar delivery points. The difference is that the time-consuming and costly part is done by the consumer on-line first; all that's left is picking up the goods.

The ultimate strategy, of course, would be *dematerialization,* a method by which the product itself would be delivered on-line. There would be no rolling warehouses, no resource pool, no delivery point. The goods purchased on-line would be delivered on-line, with the final output up to whatever computer or peripheral device is available at the consumer's receiving end.

This works for intellectual property, such as on-line books, greeting cards and music. Whether or not the consumer is ready to accept and pay for something that doesn't appear as anything other than some form of computer output, however, is another story entirely. Other considerations, such as delivery over long distances to, say, a space station or another planet, may be necessary before the value of this methodology is fully realized and embraced. But that may be a strategy for next year's supplement.

The right supply-chain strategy will depend on the nature of your company, its products and the business environment in which you operate. Dematerialization won't work, for example, with building materials, which may need the advantages of resource pooling. And logistics postponement requires all the necessary technology in order to work. When choosing to improve your supply-chain strategy, make sure you choose the right strategy for your operation. Picking the wrong one could be worse than having no strategy at all.

Mastering Supply-chain Management

The Web provides wonderful access to goods and services, but companies have to come to the table prepared to meet the rigors of that changing marketplace. The most basic question is whether there is a demand in the market for what your firm is trying to sell. If there is and electronic channels are both profitable and convenient, then you may be on your way to effective supply-chain management. Here are some other considerations for before and during the time that you set up shop:

- Design and factor costs for your supply chain before talking to other system suppliers. Developing a system based on what you need, not on what they can or choose to provide, will yield better results.
- Build a system that is an extension of your existing back-office system. First and foremost, you'll save time and money. Moreover, you don't want a system that doesn't intrinsically link to your existing operation. That just wouldn't make sense.
- Track orders from the moment they arrive and make sure they are fed into the delivery pipeline immediately. This tracking should be automatic and should link to all facets of your operation. This includes an automatic log into accounts receivable to track income, links to the warehouse to track outgo and, of course, shipment and delivery so the truckers know what they're delivering to whom and by when.

DRILLDOWN

In addition to fulfillment, the e-marketplace brings other advantages to both buyers and sellers who do business on-line. In both cases, each sees greater abilities to search out information and resources as a huge advantage of e-commerce. Global reach for both goods and services is now within everyone's grasp. Products and programs can be personalized, which leads to stronger customer relationships in some cases and greater value through higher satisfaction levels in others. Global reach also leads to more competitive and ultimately greater selection and better prices. And when the electronic supply chain does what it's supposed to do, the less costly, more efficient delivery time is simply the ribbon on the package.

- Plan peak season strategies ahead of time and make sure all company departments and, most importantly, third-party vendors are in sync, on-line and ready and able to meet the demand.

- Finally, use your system as an analysis tool to track process and progress and measure performance levels. The supply chain is only as effective as the satisfaction it brings to customers. If what you've got isn't what the customer wants, then it's back to the drawing board for you and for every other link in the chain.

Chapter S11
Wising Up to Smart Cards

You've got to hand it to the French. In addition to introducing the world to high culture, they help us think in ways that otherwise might raise an eyebrow or two. Thanks to them, we're eating escargot with relish—or at least drawn butter—and watched Jerry Lewis films (the ones without Dean Martin) with a whole new level of appreciation. And their development, acceptance and use of smart cards decades ago make North American consumers and financial service providers look positively barbaric. Of course, the French tend to think that about us anyway.

When it comes to financial transactions, it's all about cost, convenience and service. Smart cards—those little plastic rectangles colloquially known as a "computer in a credit card"—have won rave reviews in Europe and Asia. But they have barely scratched the surface here, something that has less to do with the services they provide and more to do with the price of becoming a player.

Plainly put, while the cost of consumer involvement in the smart card revolution tends to be reasonable to the point of being ridiculously cheap, the infrastructure from the merchant and provider side can be enormously expensive. Some experts estimate that the price of admission to the smart card universe could equal as much as $11 billion. Of that, the card issuers would have to absorb $4 billion to pay for their end of the processing hardware, software and card issuance. Merchants and others who accept the cards would be responsible for the remaining $7 billion. In their eyes, that's an awful lot of money to merely offer one more payment option.

But things, as they say, are changing. The emergence of smart card variations—stored-value cards that allow you to make a phone call or photocopies, deducting the cost of each from the amount stored on the cards—is helping. These seemingly innocent tools are pushing us all toward the day when we have a single card that lists everything from our bank balances and driver's license number to passport information and the list of medications we take. We may not be ready yet to jump into the future of financial transactions, but we're inching closer and closer every day.

There's also e-commerce that's helping propel us down the road. Despite the proliferation of the Internet, sales on-line still run a paltry second to brick-and-mortar merchandising. True, people like to feel the heft of the sweater, see how the sun glints off the newly waxed automobile and leaf through books and periodicals prior to purchase. But they're also still a little skittish about sending their credit card numbers out through the ether, not knowing exactly who might be in line to intercept the transmission. Built-in security devices help smart cards screen for such data leakage, making them likely tools to promote the future of Internet purchases. But we still have to get there from here.

DRILLDOWN

Like all other aspects of high-tech, the smart card industry has its own jargon and set of terms. Here are the basics that you should know:

- Smart card—Shown as either one word or two, a smart card is an integrated circuit or memory chip anywhere from 8 to 32 KB in capacity and housed in a specially designed cavity in a wallet-sized plastic rectangle that looks suspiciously like a credit card.

- Electronic purse or wallet—Although not necessarily gender-specific, the interchangeable term refers to any small portable device that stores data with monetary value.

- Stored-value card—Another name for an electronic purse or lower capacity smart card.

- Contact smart card—A smart card that transmits data through physical contact with a card reader. Think of the card swipe mechanism for magnetic stripe credit cards.

- Contactless smart card—A smart card that communicates via a tiny antenna imbedded in the card and requires no physical contact for the data to be read.

- Security access module—Another name for a smart card reader, specifically the reader's microprocessor unit that authenticates the cardholder's identity.

Fortunately—and this is assuming you're ready to embrace the technology—the future is almost here. The emphases we just discussed, coupled with the growing realization that it's time the U.S. got in touch with the '90s (or even the '80s, for that matter) and in step with the rest of the planet transactionally speaking, is on the verge of arrival. Analyst group Ovum, Inc. predicts that since the influence of smart card development has begun migrating from card manufacturers to software developers and the demand for secure Internet transaction methodologies is taking the lead, the appearance and use of smart cards will surge ahead. By next year, Ovum says, there will be as many smart cards in use as there are people on the planet. While it's true this will include the phone and copier stored-value cards mentioned earlier, well, at least it's a start.

Taking Care of Business

It wasn't all that long ago—September 1999 to be exact—that the first real volley was fired in the U.S. smart card war. That's when American Express came out with Blue, its own version of the smart card. Like so much in today's world, the focus was more on marketing than technology, with an enormous hologram serving as the design focal point of the card. It was, as they say, very cool.

The hologram was the heart of this new electronic wallet, but its power and capabilities were pretty paltry compared to the ultimate possibilities then available. The hologram housed a 16 KB chip—twice what other stored-value cards hold but only half of the capacity available at the time—giving it limited capabilities in the face of a seemingly unlimited on-line universe. AmEx also stressed the security features indigenous to the technology, a factor designed to allay the fear of making on-line purchases and to give it the required competitive edge over much dumber magnetic stripe credit cards. Plus, it had a computer chip in it and that made it way cooler than your father's plastic transaction devices of yore.

How cool was it? Cool enough to attract four million orders by year-end 2000, about twice what AmEx had expected. In addition, the company gave away smart card readers free of charge to subscribers, along with offering the card interest-free for six months and with no annual fee. Only about 8 percent of cardholders ordered the readers and virtually no merchants—on-line or on-premise—had the chip readers necessary to complete transactions. But the card was cool, the ploy worked and AmEx now has Blue in the pockets of some four million consumers, half of whom were completely new customers. Will this buying public—along with the inexorable pressure of staying current—be enough to get the merchant side of the equation to fork up the predicted $11 billion to build an infrastructure? Perhaps, but it's going to take time. Lots of it.

This seeming breakthrough in smart card application takes on a slightly different tone when we realize that smart card technology was first invented by Roland Moreno in France way back in 1974 and was first implemented on a national scale there in 1985. That means smart cards predate the personal computer, not to mention the Internet. But it's the Internet, specifically e-commerce, that supporters hope will make smart cards the preferred method of taking care of e-business. The options are, so to speak, optimal and the possibilities staggering. When it comes to making the commitment...well, that's another story.

As for AmEx's effort, the jury is still out. Smart cards are a nice idea, but they don't work if the merchant isn't equipped with a smart card reader. The card giant may be hoping that public demand will drive the provider side to get the necessary hardware and software to complete the transaction. That's a noble strategy and may well work. But like everything else that, too, will take time.

DRILLDOWN

A big fear facing smart card users has to do with transaction security, which is ironic given that smart cards correctly used offer a much safer medium than your average credit cards. Would-be users fear that a card containing a person's entire life history and all vital statistics, if lost or stolen, basically would offer a wealth of information about the cardholder to the point that privacy issues would kick in and personal security would be threatened. That would be true if smart cards were no more secure than your average PC diskette or leather wallet full of cards and documents. But smart card data is fully encrypted and password protected. In order to access smart card data, you'd need not only the card but the person to which it belongs. It functions like a cell phone in that regard. It's only useful to the rightful owner, and that's true progress when it comes to personal security.

Anatomy of a Smart Card

As mentioned earlier, smart cards come in a wide range of capabilities and capacities, sporting microchips that hold anywhere from 8 to 32 KB of memory and function. In this case, bigger is better, resulting in a card that is indeed smarter. Their simpler cousins help college students pay daily expenses, right down to financing photocopies when the appropriate coinage is not available. They help riders board the Metro mass transit in Washington, D.C. and pay for phone calls the world over. And that's just the beginning.

Defining a smart card by the tasks it performs is probably the easiest way to do it, but it's really no more difficult to discuss what a smart card is in hopes of understanding and applying its many capabilities to other similar operations. As mentioned earlier, a smart card is more than a PC diskette with an extended memory and it's also more than a credit or debit card. Much more, in fact.

The "smart" part of a smart card is a microprocessor and secured memory embedded in a piece of plastic the size and shape of a credit card. The plastic vehicle, as a matter of fact, is no more than a matter of convenience and familiarity for users, who see financial transactions often as one of its primary uses. The central processing unit still stands at 8 KB of memory for most cards, but new generations have raised the bar, jumping to 16 KB and 32 KB, along with their increasing capacity and interoperability.

From a comparison standpoint, a smart card can hold up to 80 times the data of the more traditional magnetic stripe card. The embedded semiconductor chip—the heart of the card and its raison d'être—can be either a memory chip armed with nonprogrammable logic or a miniature microprocessor with its own internal memory. This allows for a variety of options and functions, including interoperability within its own data streams and program functions. Magnetic stripe cards, by comparison, merely store static data and regurgitate it on command.

Within the smart card realm, there are two primary types of cards: contact and contactless. In the first case, the microchip communicates through physical contact with the card reader. This is the equivalent of the familiar magnetic card swipe, but a little more complex. The card reader touches a conductive module on the card's surface, allowing encrypted data to be transmitted through physical contact with the reader. From an e-commerce standpoint, this would require a keyboard swipe reader to transmit cardholder information for on-line purchases.

The contactless card, on the other hand, does just what it says. An embedded antenna in the card transmits an electromagnetic signal to the card reader, accomplishing the same data transfer without the need for physical contact. Interfaces from "fast cards," generally mounted on your car and used to pass through highway toll booths without having to stop, tend to be, if you'll pardon the pun, the primary usage currently driving the development of this technology.

The point of contact, even in remote cases, performs the secondary function of charging the card's power source. Remember, these cards do not plug in somewhere to be recharged. They don't come equipped with batteries. Microwave frequencies through which the data is transmitted also serve to feed power back to the card itself, enabling its continued function. This happens each time the card comes in contact with the reader and is critical to its continued applicability.

There's a third category of cards, often lumped together but in reality two different types of devices. The hybrid contains both types of chips—a memory chip and a microprocessor, each of which also has both contact and contactless interface capabilities. The two chips rarely talk to each other, but each plays its own role in allowing the card to be used in a variety of situations and purposes.

Combi cards, on the other hand, carry only one chip, but it has both a contact and a contactless interface enabling it to communicate in both streams. The chip may be a memory chip—used primarily for data storage—or it may be a microprocessor, which allows for data manipulation and interactivity.

DRILLDOWN

Industry watchers credit smart cards' overseas success to a number of reasons, not the least of which is the higher cost of European telephone services and the technology's use as a stored-value calling card. AT&T's breakup into more competitive "Baby Bells" in the 1980s enabled U.S. merchants to continue relying on real-time phone verification of magnetic stripe credit cards while the rest of the world scrambled for new ways to reduce the cost of doing business. In the case of e-commerce, our strength became our weakness.

This transactional myopia continues, although not for lack of trying. Subsequent wide-ranging trials of stored value mechanisms, first by Visa at the 1996 Olympic Games in Atlanta, then through a joint Visa-Mastercard effort in Manhattan in 1998, met with dubious results. American Express hopes its 1999 effort with its Blue card ultimately will hit the jackpot, but wide-ranging success remains elusive.

All four types of cards are built around the same structure. The plastic card serves as the vehicle for carrying the other components. There also is an internal electronic module and a silicon integrated circuit. It's important to know that the CPU's components and memory are part of the same integrated circuit chip and are tied together with electrical components. This structure basically excludes all foreign signals and prevents them from interfering with components within the chip. This enhances the smart card's security and makes it a safer venue for the cardholder to use.

Smart Card Insecurity

When it comes to being secure, smart cards may still be the smartest alternative when compared to credit cards, checks, cash or any other transaction devices. Whether used for shopping on-line or in the stores, they offer a wider array of options and a better internal firewall to help you cover your assets. But just because they're more secure doesn't mean they're impregnable. Steps are being taken to make them so, but until that occurs, it's wise to know what you may be up against whether you're an issuer, a merchant or a mere cardholder.

- For those who know how to do it, causing an electrical disruption to the card is a little like finding a skeleton key to your private account. Electrical charges applied to the card's contact points can switch off the security modalities, giving anyone free access to whatever information the card may be holding. Sometimes this also upsets the card's internal clock mechanism and scrambles signals such that it makes it hard for either the thief or the rightful cardholder to execute further commands. Data may still be free for the taking, but delivery of that data may occur in unexpected ways.

- If that appears too sophisticated, the card may be attacked head-on. Remember that the smart part of the card is the microprocessor and/or memory chip, and it takes little more than a pocketknife to pry it from the otherwise useless plastic. The chip then can be probed for data and under the right circumstances, information can be plundered and used. Needless to say, the final execution requires someone with technical skills that extend beyond the pocketknife level.

- Another similar method would be to attack the security system head-on, firing the billions of algorithms necessary to turn the tumblers and crack the code. The number of shots can be reduced under certain circumstances by putting the card or its microprocessor under physical stress. The pressure would introduce errors into the mechanism, causing misfires in the coding sequence and reducing the number of tries necessary to crack the code. However, the information would have to be pretty valuable to go to such lengths. The average street hoodlum, finding a lost card on the street, wouldn't be able to go to all that trouble even if he or she wanted to.

- The highly sophisticated criminal may be able to back into the card's knowledge bay through reverse engineering. The proper application of corrosive substances to the chip itself could reveal the underlying circuitry that, in turn, could be recreated and its memory chip reversed, allowing access to data. Monitoring the data streams within the circuit itself, once the layers have been peeled back, is another way to reach the information.

Chip makers continue to combat these types of assaults through enhancements in cryptography and security, including the development of bonded chips that self-destruct if security is breached. New chip designs that feature false circuits and dummy components designed to confuse and mislead more sophisticated data criminals also have come into play. From a security standpoint, smart cards are still smart enough to fool the average criminal. Someone really has to want to access your data in order to make the effort worthwhile.

DRILLDOWN

The brains behind a smart card are not only in the heads of its developers. Today's smart cards have a computing power equivalent to that of a desktop PC 20 years ago, with a great deal more flexibility and portability. Even the most basic card carries an 8 KB processor that runs at 10 MHz, with 16 KB of ROM, 8 KB of electrically reprogrammable (EEPROM) nontransient storage and 512 KB of RAM. All this is packed into a chip that's just two centimeters square and housed in a plastic card 8.5 centimeters by 5.5 centimeters. And those are just basics. New cards pack even a greater punch.

The e-commerce e-quation

Like it or not, smart cards are here and are making a serious dent in all our lives. We already mentioned the "fast pass" cards drivers use to zoom through toll booths, mass transit access passes, photocopy stored-value cards and, of course, stored-value phone cards that are everywhere. Your cell phone also has a smaller format smart card, known as a Subscriber Information Module (SIM) card that governs its memory, but from an even smaller platform. Applications of all types are on the rise.

This also is true as far as usage goes. In the European market, more than 100 million telephone cards are in circulation. More than 80 million Germans have health insurance smart cards with a record of all their vital information and 22 million French people use smart cards for banking services each and every day. Across the continents, more than 50 countries have embraced the phone cards and 20 have instituted full-service electronic wallets.

What's more, as recalcitrant as North Americans have been in the past to embrace the technology, it's clear smart cards are on the way. According to Schlumberger, Ltd., one of the Big 3 French smart card manufacturers, North American distribution will have grown from 13 million in 1996 to some 543 million by 2005. Increased use as well as increased access and demand through the growing intranet and extranet channels—not to mention, of course, the Internet itself—will drive this growth. One small card in the hand ultimately will mean a giant step for consumerkind.

According to analysts, it's no longer a matter of technology, but of changing mind-sets that will increase acceptance. The growth of Net communications within corporate culture will enhance the acceptance of any delivery methodology that provides data faster, cheaper and more completely. Smart cards can do that. In fact, in the corporate environment, their use as vehicles of commerce runs secondary to that of a corporate ID and information tool. The fact that so many company IDs are now really no more than a smart card with a photo, pocket clip and/or shoelace necklace supports the point.

What it all comes down to as far as Internet commerce goes is ease of use and security of information. No transaction media is flawless, but smart cards come about as close as one can to providing safe, secure, paperless trails of sales activity that can keep cybercrooks out of your account and away from your purchaser information. The advent of contactless smart cards—those that don't require that standard mag-card swipe to transfer information—will make on-line sales not only safer, but more convenient as well.

And who's to say that some day the card won't come with its own read-out device and wireless Internet uplink so that the PC itself becomes irrelevant. Just imagine having a pocket-sized shopping bot that sidesteps hardware and software both to find the goods you need at the prices you want. By comparison, someday even the Internet could seem like old technology as your card links you straight to the source.

With smart cards, just about anything is possible.

Chapter S12

Holding Your Vendors' Feet to the Fire without Getting Burned Yourself

At the heart of any company are the people and the agreements that have gotten the operation to where it is today. Success is built on relationships between materials supplier and manufacturer, between manufacturer and seller, between seller and buyer. We all are customers of one another, links in the supply chain that delivers products and services designed to meet consumers' needs. We play our roles, we do our jobs, we meet our quotas and we make our sales. That's the season of commerce in a tidy nutshell.

Sounds good, doesn't it? Don't you wish that the system worked just like that? Sometimes, it does, and that makes everyone happy. But often it doesn't. There are problems, a supplier you've chosen doesn't perform well, and the failure is all your fault.

Does the following scenario sound familiar?

Your company has grown at a rapid rate, so much so that you needed to increase service capacity in several areas, including data processing. You're getting bigger, but are not yet big enough to install that new computer platform you've been coveting. It makes good sense to monitor this progress through several seasons and see just what the average workload will likely be and whether or not that platform really will be sufficient. But good sense is one thing; meeting current capacity needs so that you can retain that hard-won customer base is another. That will be critical to survival and has to be done.

So you signed a deal with a relatively new alternative service provider (ASP). Sure, they were untried, but they said all the right things and have the equipment necessary to support your operation. You've completed a statement of work (SOW) and signed a contract to verify that what you want to see is what you will get. Plus, because they're new, they were willing to cut you a deal and save you a significant amount of money over the competition. Since cash preservation is what you're about right now, that seemed like a safe and prudent row to hoe. So forward together arm in arm you go...or went.

Six months have passed and now you're singing a different tune. Having a SOW and a contract is all well and good, but you neglected to articulate the terms of your service-level agreement (SLA) and suddenly your ASP is dragging. Like propellerheads in a circuitry store, this group found that its eyes were bigger than its stomach and the ASP bit off a lot more contracts than it could chew, digest and swallow. You're getting the services you need and at a rate that's perfectly acceptable to your ASP, but much slower than you and your customers need them to be.

Moreover, since you chose an independent software vendor attempting to expand the service side of its business, everything has to be tried on their proprietary software first. They're eventually making most of the operations work, but not with the speed, economy or effectiveness that you need. Consequently, your own business is suffering and your board of directors is getting angry at the complaints and the fact that company growth is being offset by service decline, something you said wouldn't happen when contracting with this new ASP as a delivery partner.

Solutions? If they haven't noticed, don't tell your superiors that you neglected to get a specifically worded service-level agreement (SLA). That would have gone a long way toward solving your problems. All you can do now is look for loopholes in the contract and ways to leverage service improvements while you watch as the calendar pages agonizingly measure your contract's duration. And while you're at it, you may just want to spruce up that résumé. Like your company, you may personally find that you have rough sledding ahead.

Beyond Mere Technical Expertise

When you entered the world of computers and Internet management, it was because you were taken with the technology, intrigued by the intricacies of the on-line and off-line options, and enthused by the operating environment possibilities. It was a whole new techno world and you wanted to be part of the fun and, perhaps, thought about getting rich in the process.

You got good enough to be promoted and now you're chief technology officer. You have to know your system inside and out, not to mention all those other systems that might perform even better. Moreover, you're the designated expert witness and chief negotiator with other high-tech types who provide the services necessary to support your system. And that means occasionally holding your vendors' feet to the fire while trying not to get burned yourself.

That's been the evolution of the high-tech professional, the CTO who drives the technological train for his or her firm. It's probably not as much fun as you thought it might be, but it's even more critical to the business side of the operation than you ever dreamed. And that means that contracting, purchasing and licensing agreements all fall under your authority. You know the tech side of the business cold, but whether you're prepared for negotiations is another question entirely.

These days negotiating abilities are probably more critical to the CTO than to just about any other executive. Company fortunes rise and fall based on the firm's ability to stay competitive. After product and/or service innovation, staying competitive is the most critical factor for survival. It usually boils down to speed, accuracy and flexibility in delivery channels, all of which fall under the authority of the CTO and his or her minions. That means good business management skills, especially good negotiating skills, are as important as technological understanding. Those skills also form the foundation of vendor management strategies and are central to getting what you want when you want it and for the price you want to pay. CTOs who lack preparation in negotiations lack a critical tool in their professional arsenal, one on which the fate of their enterprise and their livelihood depends.

Not to mention, of course, their job security and the future of their careers.

Negotiation by Definition

Few people enjoy confrontation, especially when high stakes are involved. Professional athletes know the fate of the game depends on their ability to continually excel. Attorneys know their clients will go free only if they can confront the situation and turn opinion to their advantage. Surgeons understand the very lives of their patients rest in their understanding of the medical condition and their skill in its surgical treatment. In all cases, advanced negotiations—in either facing resistance from opponents, managing the situations themselves or battling perceived limitations within themselves—could literally change or save lives.

Negotiations with your IT vendors don't quite have the same life-or-death ramifications, but they still are critical to your twin goals of maximizing vendor performance while minimizing cost. Those are the goals that govern any business operation and help contribute to the net margin. Your operations head seeks to keep costs low, while marketing attempts to generate sales and make profits high. Even your chief financial officer is in charge of the company's investments, making sure that yield from daily, weekly and longer-term returns are all they can be. That's part of their job, just as negotiating with high-tech vendors is part of the CTO's job.

Unless we've received specific training or experience, many of us run from the idea of having to negotiate big-dollar contracts. But if you've ever purchased anything of any size—a house, a car, a boat or perhaps even a sizeable home computer system—then you've been exposed to negotiations. Even the relationships in your life are the result of effective negotiations with friends and loved ones, bargaining what you have to offer to get what you need in return. Negotiations form the heart of human relations. It's a fact of life, as well as part of the human condition. We all do it to some degree every day. Even CTOs.

Negotiations have gone on since the beginning of recorded history. The word *negotiate,* from the Latin word *negotiatus,* is defined by Webster's *New World Dictionary* as:

> *to confer, bargain or discuss with a view to reaching agreement; to make arrangements for or settle a business transaction or treaty; to succeed in crossing, surmounting or moving through (as in to negotiate a river).*

No doubt the definition of the word doesn't surprise you. But consider the subtleties of the language used in that definition and you'll understand more of the nuances of what we're talking about. The first half of the definition stresses ways to "reach an agreement," rather than emphasizing the negotiator's role in overcoming an opponent or foe. This is a critical part of successful negotiations that we'll discuss later in this chapter.

The second half of the definition references the negotiator's ability to surmount hurdles and overcome obstacles. That, too, is an intrinsic part of the definition. Obstacles are obstacles until they are overcome and that generally happens through successful negotiations. That aspect, too, will be discussed later. It's important to note that both of those nuances say nothing about conflict or struggle.

At its best, negotiation becomes an exercise in problem solving, the results of which should benefit all parties involved in the process. Despite what some people think, negotiation correctly done can be an enjoyable exercise that tests the limits of both the situation and the principals involved in the process. Of course, it doesn't always work out that way, especially when you're facing someone who doesn't really understand the true nature of negotiation. Your best intentions still could devolve into a struggle in which no one really wins and no needs are served. However, if you come to the table prepared and can skillfully use the elements of good negotiation despite the level of sophistication or the lack thereof that you face, then half the battle has been won.

More to the point, if you know what you're doing and your vendor doesn't, you'll have a much better chance of holding his or her feet to the fire without getting burned.

DRILLDOWN

Before you begin negotiations, identify first-, second- and third-level goals not only from a fallback position, but as part of an overall developmental strategy. You may go in with an ideal goal and walk away with a few concessions to an existing relationship. If those concessions are identified and directed strategically, then you may be equally as well off or perhaps even better off than if the ideal goal had required costly concessions on your part.

Some veteran negotiators go in with a much grander goal than they hope to achieve. Their true objective is really a series of concessions that better suit their operational or financial needs without incurring additional costs. In addition, your opponent walks away feeling that he's succeeded, perhaps even with the perception of beating you at your own game. Think of the last time you bought a car. You paid an amount closer to what the salesperson wanted than what you wanted, but you got the free wheel covers, right? That was an example of this strategy being used against you with great success.

The Foundation of Negotiation

Some of us are born blondes, some brunettes, others redheads. None of us are born negotiators, and that's the first thing to remember. Negotiation skills are just that—skills learned through intellectual understanding, situational application and practice, practice, practice. Some of us are born extroverts, and the extrovert's need to talk makes that person seem like a born negotiator. Nothing could be further from the truth. Negotiation is much like a dance, with each party taking turns directing the progress through subtle and not-so-subtle strategies and actions. Extroverts who always insist on leading don't dance very well for very long and eventually may find themselves without a dance partner.

The heart of good negotiation is neither the fast-talking sales approach nor the Japanese method of "thick face, black heart," which relies on silence and inscrutability. Both those skills come into play, but the foundation of successful negotiation is preparation, preparation and, when that fails, preparation. The negotiator who enters the arena unprepared will soon be lost. It then becomes a matter of how much loss and at what speed. More simply put, know what you want, what you don't want, what you can afford and when you need to walk away. Even if you prepare only at that most rudimentary level, you will be better equipped than most of the untrained negotiators you will face.

Know thyself is one of the best credos a negotiator can have and, for as complex as each of us is, knowing yourself for the purpose of most negotiation is alarmingly simple. So simple, in fact, that people often try to second-guess themselves and complicate things just because they think they should. Resist that temptation. Before any negotiation, take a deep breath and understand what each of the following means to you:

Clearly understand the goals and desired outcome of your negotiations.

You'll never reach your goal if you don't know what that goal is. If you can do nothing else, identify what it is you'd like to come out of the proceedings, what your ideal result will be. Gear your words and actions toward achieving that result and then be ready to move forward. Most of us don't achieve the ideal, but the results tend to be a lot more satisfying if our reach exceeds our grasp. That works in negotiation just like it does elsewhere. Perhaps even better.

But please note: You have to believe in the worth of that goal if you're going to negotiate successfully. Your efforts to pursue a raise must be based on past accomplishments that warrant the increase, not just your desire to have more money. If you'd like your client company to serve as a beta site for your latest software iteration, you'll need both rationale and benefit in order for the idea to make sense. Before you set your goal, make sure your discussion platform or purpose is rock-solid. That will go a long way in supporting your efforts.

Set milestones before you begin to negotiate.

You already know what your ideal deal will be. That's the goal you built from the platform of purpose you established. But unless your position is ironclad, your offer completely in sync with everyone's goals and your skills honed to a razor's edge, you're not going to get there in one jump. If you haven't planned out the steps you need to take and the milestones you need to hit in the process, your efforts will be derailed at the first bump in the road.

When negotiating for a complex service package, for example, you know that it will be done as a series of steps. Each may constitute its own negotiation, or it may be negotiable as part of the overall package. Either way, you'll need to work through all the components, carefully working your way toward the ultimate goal. Failure to pay attention to the component parts can undermine the effort as a whole. Give each its due relative to its importance to your goals and objectives, but don't ignore any. Negotiations could break down or fail entirely based on one small stone left unturned.

Know the difference between what you want and what you'll accept.

This may translate into varying degrees of your goal, or a set of alternate goals that will become an acceptable alternative and outcome to your negotiation. Remember, negotiation is the act of arriving at a mutually beneficial outcome to a discussion or issue facing you or your company. Your secondary goal may not constitute the most desirable outcome, but it's probably better than no goal at all if it means negotiations will fail entirely.

Let's take this to a personal level and apply it to your next salary nego-tiations. You want *x* amount of money and make your case based on the con-tributions you've made to the firm. They are considerable and you truly believe you deserve the amount. The Big Boss notes that company earnings overall are down and that your innovations, while a nice addition to the serv-ice profile, haven't done quite enough to improve efficiency or increase prof-itability. They may have significant financial impact someday but, until that time, there is a wage freeze on and you'll have to be content with your cur-rent salary. The Big Boss was very nice about it, but that was as definitive a turndown as you have ever received.

If you have no secondary goals in mind, your choice is to a) passively accept the rejection and go back to work, perhaps letting the boss know that you're more of a pushover than was first thought; or b) stick to your guns and resign your position. If what the Big Boss says is true, there may be nothing any-one can or will do about it. You've won in principle but lost in practice. Either way, you didn't achieve your goal, which was financial more than philosophical.

However, if you've set secondary goals that have value to you, you may walk away a winner, while the Big Boss gains from having met the needs and desires of a valuable employee. If there's no money for raises, perhaps they will let you gain additional value through increased vacation time or flextime that allows you to do some work from home, or let you attend the workshop or conference that you've been wanting to go to for the past two years. (That money comes out of another pot.) Perhaps you'll be allowed to take on more responsibility, increasing your value to the firm and enabling you to earn more now or at some later specified date. Whatever your secondary goal may be, it can be a fallback position that enables you to succeed in your negotiation efforts. In a case like this, sometimes achieving success for its own sake can be critical for your continued career advancement.

Prepare thoroughly or proceed ineffectively.

We shouldn't have to say this, but there is always someone who doesn't real-ize that the need to prepare for any negotiation is the secret to success. It doesn't matter if you're buying a car, negotiating for a companywide IT sys-tem or getting ready to propose marriage to that special someone. The amount of planning for the negotiation done beforehand operates in corresponding proportion to the rate of success. In this case, we're talking about two types of planning you should pursue:

- Do your homework. If you're going to negotiate for a new platform, for example, understand your company's needs and know beforehand how the system meets those needs. In detail. This seems basic to the point of being obvious, but our busy lives cause us to pass over details and reinterpret basics to fill in the knowledge gaps so that we can get on to other, more pressing tasks. Homework done beforehand, thorough to the point that it needs to be in order to answer the questions you're going to ask, will save you time and energy during the negotiation process. It also will make you a better negotiator because you will know in detail what you're dealing with and your efforts will be directed to addressing the strengths and weaknesses of both the product and the position, not learning about them for the first time. The less control your opponent believes he or she has, the straighter the discussion will be and the better the result will be for you.

- Organize yourself. This is as basic as making sure you have all the right notes and background data and making sure you are mentally prepared to negotiate. Well-organized documents are easily accessible and physically display the fact that you have, indeed, done your homework and are ready to discuss the issue completely and intelligently. In an extended sense, your effort also communicates the fact that you value the other person's time and want to make the negotiation both thorough and effective. Once again, it makes you a better negotiator because you not only are prepared, but you appear prepared. And as we all know, your opponent's perception often becomes reality.

It's also important to be organized intellectually and emotionally before going into negotiation. As we said earlier, this is a learned skill set that takes practice. If you have done your lessons well, then you have the tools at ready disposal and can use them as appropriate steps in the process. Make sure, too, that you are emotionally prepared for the confrontation. If you were just informed that your spouse is leaving you or that your brother is in jail, chances are you will not be emotionally sober enough to proceed. If the going gets tough, you may erupt for the wrong reasons, damaging your position and compromising your goal. One of the greatest negotiating skills is knowing when to postpone negotiations. Don't be afraid to use it for good reason.

Good preparation and a positive mental and emotional attitude are sometimes all you need to out-negotiate the opposition. At the very least, the combination forms a good foundation from which to take action.

DRILLDOWN

Negotiations often result in contracts which, by their nature, provide precise articulation of terms and conditions. Bring a similar level of care to your negotiation proceedings and you will be way ahead of the game. If you're negotiating with an ASP for "dependable, timely service," have them define what dependable and timely mean to them to make sure that they meet your expectation. Know, too, what the terms need to mean to you; otherwise, you're likely to accept their definition. Documentation that supports this need for precision—and the creation of documentation, or at least notes where none exists—should be a critical part of your negotiating strategy. You won't get what you need unless you ask for it precisely. And you won't be able to ask for it precisely if you don't fully understand what you're looking for in the first place.

Preparing to Meet Your Opponent

When it comes to negotiation, preparing your own resources is half the battle. The other half comes from learning all you can about your opponent in the process. We use the term "opponent" carefully because it implies opposition. In most cases, that's how negotiations start. By the end, if the negotiations have been conducted successfully, that opponent could well become your newest business partner. It's up to the two of you to make that happen. For the time being, we'll continue to use the term "opponent" as a way to reinforce that lesson.

Presumably, you've done all you can to research the object of the negotiations as well as search your soul and that of your firm to understand what it means to you and the role it needs to play in your operational and financial future. Now it's time to know your opponent as well as you know yourself. This will be a lot tougher than the first half of the assignment, especially since much of what you need to know constitutes proprietary information or operates at a knowledge level that won't become clear until you are well into negotiations.

Nevertheless, there is much that can and should be done in getting to know who you will be negotiating with over the next hour, day, week or month. That knowledge operates at two specific levels:

- In the case of business-to-business negotiation, quite obviously, you'll need to know the company, its products and its market and financial position. In the case of a publicly held company, there is a wide array of information available at the surface, all of which is very helpful. Rely only on that, however, and you will miss critical organizational patterns, plans and needs that really form the crux of your negotiation intelligence. Start broad, but dig as deep as you can before building your opponent's company profile.

- You also will need to know the negotiators and who the decision maker really is. It's the decision maker to whom you ultimately will need to address your negotiating advances. Some firms hire professionals to negotiate or create screen players who collect critical data, assess options and then report their findings with recommendations back to the decision maker for evaluation.

  What seems at first like faulty logic is really a negotiating strategy that, in the right hands, can be very effective. The unsuspecting negotiator can be expertly manipulated and set up, only to be knocked gently over by the Big Boss when he or she comes in to deliver the killing stroke. Be wary of such situations and establish early whose name will be signed on the contract's dotted line. Then minimize your efforts and the information you share with the flak-catchers and hired guns until such time as you can meet face-to-face with the Big Boss.

Once you know who you'll be dealing with, you'll be better able to create an effective strategy. Glean all you can about the company and the individual from trade publications, industry associations, the local library and other sources. If the company is publicly held, Standard & Poor's can give you a good sense of their financial position relative to their competition. Also, don't be afraid to ask competitors and other customers about their experiences and impressions. Industry intelligence always starts at the grassroots level and trades up, often being amplified or sanitized on the way. Understand the perspectives of the opinions you receive, as well as their contexts, then mix it all together. A composite picture should emerge. Use that composite to compose your negotiation strategy.

To this point, much of what we've described has taken on a tone of opposition, as if setting the stage to do battle. There is some element of that, as we said, to many negotiations. But stressing that too strongly might cause you to hunker down and prepare to fight. A good negotiator takes a more sophisticated approach and looks for a way that both sides can walk away from the process as winners. You can do this by exploring what motivates your opponents, then developing arguments that equalize the opposition and enhance the positives.

This is not difficult to do. However, it's not a step that should be taken lightly. You have no doubt created stacks of files and inches of information to support your own argument. You also should set aside the time to physically list the characteristics, traits and goals of your opponents to see how they match with yours. This may be as simple as listing your goals next to those of your opponent and seeing where they line up. This then can serve as the foundation to your negotiations, topics on which you already believe you agree. Once this has been ascertained, together you can move on to address the more difficult issues.

Of course, there always will be areas where things go awry. Either you or your opponent will make assertions that, if left unchecked or unaddressed, will become potent weapons as the negotiation proceeds. Like moves in a chess game, you can't afford to leave these hanging issues unchecked. Concerted efforts should be made to at least equalize or, at best, neutralize their impact. This often takes the course of countering an assertion with one you know to be more factual, or at least one that spins more in your favor. That will keep you on even ground, perhaps propel you ahead, but help you both work more toward a joint and equitable conclusion.

Here are three ways to equalize your opponent's statements:

Fully explore and articulate your opponent's claims.

As mentioned earlier, negotiations often are emotional discourse disguised as intellectual discussion. As such, broad, sweeping assertions often come into play and, if left unchecked, quickly become fact. You can equalize claims that the new computer system for which you're negotiating is far superior to other models by reviewing all the features and benefits. You'll likely discover that, while the new system does have some engaging features and offers higher levels of performance, there are areas in which it just doesn't measure up to what else is on the market. Were you to purchase such a system, there would be some serious customization and upgrade issues that would have to come as part of the price.

Demonstrate that your opponent's position is irrelevant or inaccurate.

Similar to the above situation, there will be times when you need to point out hyperbole and personal prejudice for what it is within the context of negotiations. Your self-esteem and congratulations on a job well done in your pursuit of a raise had better be balanced by reality. The last thing you want is for the Big Boss to point out that, while you were busy designing the new system that someday may be useful, order fulfillment time increased and productivity and revenue dropped as a result. Your opponent may try similar tactics, sometimes innocently or unknowingly. It behooves you to be sure these impressions are corrected in everyone's mind. Otherwise, any inaccuracies will come back later to bite you.

Offset your opponent's assertions by putting forward your own, more accurate positions.

That superior new computer platform you're negotiating for is going to take a lot of staff time and effort on your part to make sure its compatible and operational with your own legacy systems still operating. That may not be your opponent's fault, but that certainly is a consideration that you have and around which you will make your purchasing decision. Your opponent's failure to recognize that impact could cost you significant dollars. The other firm's unwillingness to compromise to meet your needs may tell you all you need to know about whether or not—emphasis on "not"—to make the purchase.

Equalizing arguments is a key negotiation strategy and one of which it's worth taking special note. Some veteran negotiating teams have members who do nothing but listen for platitudes, promises and falsehoods with the idea of creating equalization strategies. If you can't commit someone full-time, at least sensitize yourself so that you're ready to respond when they come up. And they will come up.

> ### DRILLDOWN
>
> When it comes to negotiating, your body language says as much or more about your position as the words you use and the tone in which you speak. The Japanese have a phrase, "thick face, black heart," that speaks to this very thing. Japanese negotiators try to make their faces 'thick"—you might be more familiar with the term "poker face"—so that opponents don't see any trace of human emotion or response to the progress of the negotiation. In the same way, by "blackening" their hearts, they don't let anything other than the process of the negotiation and terms of the agreement get into their thoughts or feelings. You say your dog was just run over by a bus? Unless we're negotiating a pet food account, that fact and its attendant emotions have no business here.
>
> That approach may be a little extreme, but it speaks to the point. If you're in the middle of tense negotiations, don't telegraph your position through a scowl on your face or arms tightly folded across your chest. It may give your opponents the informational advantage for which they're looking and they may leverage that position without you ever having said a word.

Time to Negotiate

Preparation is important and you'll know how well you planned when it comes time to negotiate. That's the trial by fire and the only way you'll know whether your negotiating skills are up to par. However, if you've done your homework, prepared mentally and emotionally for conflict, believe in your position and the platform supporting it, have secondary goals in mind and—very important—know when to walk away, you should be set to make the most of your problem-solving exercise.

And remember, this can be fun if you let it be. So, let it be and let's begin.

Set the time and place to meet your needs, not those of your opponent.

Professional athletes know that there is such a thing as a home-field advantage. Never negotiate in the office of your opponent or, if possible, anywhere on company premises. That will be his or her power spot and may gain your opponent significant psychological advantage by operating there.

The mark of a neophyte negotiator is offering the opposition choice of venue and time of meeting. Be the first to suggest a location—your office may be best for you, although a neutral place like a restaurant or even a park brings its own advantages. Pick a time when you're at your peak. Are you a morning person? Then 4 o'clock in the afternoon would probably be a bad choice. Go with your strengths and give a reasonable rationale for your choice. By being first to speak and choosing the time and place, you've already set negotiations in motion. That puts you in the driver's seat, which is where you want to be.

Find a common ground and a positive note on which you can start.

Small talk has its purpose. Skillfully done, casual questions about the opponent's likes, dislikes, interests and families can be used to judge character and find a bond on which you can build. Perhaps you both have teenage daughters or a six-stroke handicap. Such commonalities are positive characteristics that you share, things that make you more like each other. A skillful negotiator knows that this will contribute to the bonding that ultimately will be helpful in swaying the opponent in your direction.

Remember once again that despite our continued use of the word "opponent" and continued emphasis on cultivating your advantage, the best negotiations are win–win situations in which both parties walk away satisfied that each got the best deal possible. Small talk does more to work toward this end than you would believe.

Transfer your preparation into evidence and support materials.

Earlier we stressed the importance of preparing for the negotiation. Now it's time to march the by-products of that preparation out and on to the negotiating table. Your opponent will know you've prepared by all the facts, data and assumptions you've accumulated and developed prior to the meeting. Make sure you show the fruits of your labor: notes, files, graphs and charts, data, opinions, survey results.

Whatever you have needs to be neatly sorted and made available for your consultation during the negotiations. Certainly, it will aid you in making your case. But the presence of that material—as long as it's easily accessible and not presented in a disheveled jumble—will impress your opponent with both your seriousness and grasp of the subject.

Maintain your edge and call time if you lose your advantage.

Negotiating is tough work and you have to be mentally and emotionally prepared to face your opponent. If at any time you feel yourself slipping or losing your sense of timing, call for a time-out and do what's necessary to get your focus back on the subject at hand. This may require something as minor as a trip to the rest room or a drink of water. If it's a little more serious, you may want to recess until after lunch or, if it's late in the day, call it quits until the following morning.

You may even need to suspend negotiations until later that week. Just like walking away from a deal, walking away from the negotiating table when your light is burning low is better than losing the negotiation and accepting terms with which you can't live. Novice negotiators fear that suspending negotiations is a sign of weakness. The pros know that's merely a maneuver and may purposely do it to gain strategic advantage. Use it wisely and it can become a very effective tool to keep the opponent off guard and guessing about your next move.

Question carefully and for strategic advantage.

Questioning is one of the most effective negotiating tools. In addition to uncovering necessary information, questions can drill down to levels that your opponent hadn't originally intended to expose. Ask the right questions and you'll have the information you need to get the results you want.

A good questioner often can lead an opponent in the direction you want to go, driving toward agreement ("You really like the color of that car's upholstery, don't you?"), all of which adds to the ultimate goal of getting the opponent to say yes to your demands. General questions are best asked in the beginning to help direct the flow of conversation. Save specific questions for a little later on when you need to win points or overcome hurdles. Remember that the more times your opponent says yes, even to obvious questions, the better his mood and the easier it is to sway him in your direction.

Build your case slowly and remember that patience isn't only a virtue, it's a strategy.

Those uncomfortable with the negotiating process want nothing more than to end it as quickly as possible. You know you have the upper hand when an opponent says she "just wants to get this over with" or "thinks that we can arrive at the right conclusion quickly and painlessly." That's when you settle back, draw in and take all the time you need. Chances are your opponent will slip and show her hand early, then become an ally—either willing or unwilling—in helping you accomplish your goals.

Build your case from the bottom up and negotiate one point at a time. In a complex deal there are often several key components in play at once—price, product specifications and delivery time, for example. If your case is strong and you're the master of your facts, you can juggle these balls from time to time to keep your opponent off guard. You're interested in a favorable conclusion on each, but you don't need to close them methodically, one at a time. Once can be used as a diversionary tactic for the other, for example, and you can manipulate your opponent's emotions by refusing his offer to close on one in favor of discussing another. By the time your opponent finally has a grasp of the situation, chances are it's the grasp you want him to have. Then go for the close of all three or one at a time, making sure the answer you get is the one you want.

Know your opponent as you would know yourself.

The world is full of people, each as different as the next. But most if not all tend to fall into a manageable number of personality types. Knowing whether you're dealing with a Type A hard charger or a consensus-seeking touchy-feely kind of person will make a difference in the way you approach him or her. Part of your small talk exercise is to uncover these characteristics and be prepared for what prejudices and preferences your opponent will bring to the table. Techniques that work well with one type absolutely will fail with another. Are hard numbers or a gut feeling going to be the deciding factor in leading this person to saying yes? Using the right strategy with the wrong person can lead to dreadful results.

This is too complex a topic to discuss within the confines of this chapter. As you hone your negotiating skills, you may want to look for more complete information on personality types and decide which ones you are most likely to run across. Knowing your opponent—or at least his or her psychological type—as well as you know yourself is a key factor in successful negotiations.

Stay on course.

One of the most difficult things to do during negotiations is to stay focused and operate based on the cumulative knowledge you have acquired during your discussion. Part of this is human nature. Buddhists call this "monkey mind," the habit of your consciousness to tire of being disciplined and hop around from topic to topic. Unless this is a deflection tactic and part of a larger disarming strategy, lack of mental discipline could lead to the dulling of your negotiating edge.

Part of this habit, too, has to do with fear of failure and avoidance of conflict. Ongoing negotiations require an intellectual acuity similar to those exercised by chess champions, always trying to play one step ahead of their opponents. But it also strikes at the heart of personal values and worth, mixing in

DRILLDOWN

Emotions sometimes run high during negotiations and tempers have been known to flare. But keep in mind that the negotiator who gets truly angry has lost the argument. Anger is an emotional release and, as such, results in a loss of control. If your opponent has gone beyond the point of anger, he or she has lost the edge, putting you in the driver's seat.

Some negotiators, however, use controlled anger to put their opponents on edge. The purpose of controlled anger, of course, is to upset the opponent's balance, causing a loss of edge, or to deflect attention from the current issue, so it can be brought up later in a way more advantageous to the negotiator. Sometimes anger begets anger, causing you to vent your true feelings and hand the advantage over to the other person.

In the face of anger during negotiations, the best thing you can do is keep cool and retain control. You gain nothing and stand to lose everything if you get angry. Dissect the problem and attempt to identify exactly what has angered your opponent. If it can be remedied with no loss of edge for yourself, do so immediately and get on with negotiations. If it runs deeper, recess your negotiations until such time as both parties can come together again with cool heads.

emotions at the most inconvenient times and places. This, too, is the result of human nature.

The best strategy to help you stay on course during negotiations is to practice mental discipline and emotional sobriety whenever and wherever possible. That way, both tools will be at your disposal automatically when you need them.

Asking Technology Vendors the Hard Questions

When it comes specifically to dealing with technology vendors—ASPs are the most common—good service boils down to compatibility. If you're contracting with an ASP, ISP or any other provider, you must know that your system can talk to their system and do so with a minimum of interference, hassles and downtime. As we said earlier, this requires a solid technical background (to know what you're talking about) and comprehensive business savvy (so you know how to talk about it). Some understanding of the competition and the nature of the human creature helps as well. Granted, that's a tall order, but it's something CTOs and other technocrats do and do successfully every day.

But you can do it if you keep in mind the four cornerstones of any high-tech negotiations: technological capabilities, service profile, business practices, and pricing.

- Technological capabilities speak to the vendor's architecture and communications capability. If the firm is operating off an old or antiquated mainframe, then there's something wrong with the picture, in terms of either technological sophistication—they may not have enough—or financial stability—once again, they may not have enough. Would you run your business on such a system? If not, should you partner with or rely on someone who does?

- The service profile talks not only to what they're willing to do for you, but what they are capable of doing for anyone, including themselves. Do they speak multiple languages in variable formats? Can they grow with your needs, in terms of both capacity and sophistication? Will you be in charge of helping to finance significant upgrades in the near future?

- Business practice is an area too often ignored, but one that shouldn't be underestimated. To provide acceptable service to you or anyone else requires that the vendor be successful on the business side of the equation. If they can't manage their own shop, they certainly can't help you manage yours. This includes everything from office and facilities to financial stability. Look at them as if they were a company you wanted to buy, not just buy services from, and you'll get a better perspective of their business acumen and whether you should be doing business with them.

- Pricing, on the other hand, too often becomes the focal point of negotiations. Getting the right price from the wrong company is a lot like using grocery store coupons for products you don't really want. Focus on value, rather than price. In addition to bringing the other three factors under consideration, the value focus will help you wind up where you want to be and get more of what you've paid for.

Demand a Well-written SLA

In the high-tech world, a well-written service-level agreement (SLA) is worth its weight in microchips. A statement of work (SOW) and a contract to enforce that agreement are critical, but the SLA is the real workhorse, the make-or-break document that will determine whether you get what you want when you want it, or something entirely different delivered in someone else's own sweet time.

SLAs, which should define performance metrics in clear, easy-to-understand language, have been both the boon and bane of high-tech operations and some companies' very existence. The problem tends not to be with the document's intent so much as the language, terms and conditions listed. An SLA, after all, is a legal contract and what it says is what will be expected in terms of performance standards. If the SLA doesn't clearly articulate expectations, then anything roughly approximating the agreement is suitable. That's how contracts work and that's a characteristic of which you should be wary.

At a minimum, your SLA should identify minimum bandwidth and its availability at which times during the day. It should identify acceptable quality of service (QOS) levels and discuss downtime and its ramifications. Most of all, it should address damages in the event all or some of these promises fail. Financial compensation in the form of service fee reductions is one thing, breaking of the contract something else. But if you lose customers due to extensive downtime, there is often no way to measure the extent of that damage. In this case, financial damages also may be involved.

When it comes to pricing, look for competitive costs but be wary of vendors priced significantly below market. Something is going on here and it may be no more than a loss-leader rate to get into the industry or your firm in hopes of making up the loss through an increase of business in the future. On the other hand, this may be a vendor who truly doesn't have the capability to meet your needs, operates with outdated technology that will let you down, or has some other intrinsic problem that will cause you heartburn in the near future. Even in the technology world, you still get what you pay for. Again, remember that value rather than price should be the determining factor.

Once you've negotiated the best SLA you can, the first part of the exercise has been completed. Now it will be up to you to monitor performance closely to make sure you're getting exactly what you paid for. An SLA, like any contract, is a promissory note for services to come. However, even the best of intentions are sometimes compromised. Just because you have it in writing doesn't mean it's going to happen. Monitoring progress will give added insight, both for current operations as well as future negotiations, and you'll be better able to head off trouble before it strikes.

Finally, follow up every SLA with a pilot project designed to test the agreement you just signed. You won't know for certain whether the terms to which you agreed can be executed successfully and successively until you test the process. What sounded good in concept may be an absolute disaster in practice. You won't want to be tied to that practice or have to make significant financial concessions to change it once you've found out the hard way. That's the key purpose behind a pilot. Make sure the SLA is contingent on the success of that pilot so you aren't hung with services or terms you don't want or can't use.

But be realistic about results. All processes require a certain margin for error. That's only fair to the vendor (not to mention that you can drive yourself crazy seeking a level of perfection that is unattainable). Decide early whether that margin is 5 percent or 10 percent. Anything less might be too unrealistic; anything more will be damaging to your customer service profile. Make that part of the SLA, too.

Don't forget, too, that the basics of good negotiations we discussed earlier come into play throughout the process. It doesn't matter if you're negotiating with an ASP for the purchase of a new platform, or to get yourself the raise you no doubt deserve. Negotiations require preparation, planning and research. In addition, you have to know the capabilities and "hot buttons" of your opponents as well as understanding your own strengths and weaknesses. Know where you're willing to compromise and where you must stand firm. Understand your strengths and use them to negotiate for what you want when you want it and under what terms it should be delivered.

Once you can do that, you're head and shoulders above everyone else, including your competition, in defining your market advantage. And then you will deserve that raise. What's more, you'll have all the skills you need to make sure that you get it.

DRILLDOWN

Successful negotiations are based on the terms and conditions of your agreement with the vendor in question. Some negotiate better than others and vendors don't want to hand an unnecessary advantage to the next novice negotiator who walks through their doors. That's why many of them insist on nondisclosure agreements that restrict you from telling the next guy down the block how good a deal you really got, under penalty of lawsuit.

The agreement protects the vendor from having to match prices, and it also keeps you from discovering whether or not someone else got a better deal. There's nothing you could do after the fact anyway. Assuming you've employed all the negotiating skills in your power and bargained for value as well as service, you no doubt got what you needed and wanted.

Chapter S13
Weaving the Holistic Web

With apologies to Walt Disney, it's a Web world, after all.

And there's no little irony in that assertion. As the Web as an entity and a social engine grows more influential, more pervasive and more essential to our daily lives, the Web as a tool gets more intimate, more immediate and more manageable to the individuals who use it. And these days just about anyone still able to draw a breath is on-line.

What makes the Web even more critical is the role it plays with new generations, those who see the technology as anything but a mere tool. To those who grew up in its shadow, it's an essential life force, a connection to others and to other worlds. It has a life of its own and a capability to expand our lives beyond their meager existence and, through electronic capabilities, enhance personal skills, abilities and resources such that some Netheads think they could not exist without Web access. And for some of them, that's not far from the truth.

What that means is greater and greater dependence on the Web, not merely as a business tool or commercial outlet, but as something that contributes intrinsically to the very existence of its users. The Web becomes a force that is certainly part of their intellect, probably part of their emotions and possibly even part of their soul. For them, there are no "what ifs" about the Web, only "whens" and "why not nows?"

Heady stuff? Maybe, but there's a percentage of you who probably don't think so, and among that group another percentage who can't believe the myopia and limited view such comments reflect. And there's even a group who knows that, should you want to, you can make all that I just said a reality by going on-line and declaring it so. Veteran marketers know that perception is reality. The Web has expanded the concept of perception, entwining it with rapid-fire, uncontrolled public opinion. Pitchforks and torches time, if you will.

If you want a product to sell, a concept to develop or an ideology to be embraced, you simply tell each other so through various Web discussion channels, thus changing reality as we know it. According to the authors of *The Cluetrain Manifesto,* you already do that on a daily basis. The future will hold more, not less, of the same.

What other issues are coming down the road that will have a profound impact on Web technology? We can't even begin to discuss them in quantity. Some already are here, however, and in terms of their trajectory and impact, it's just a matter of degree before they become a part of all our lives. Consider some of the following as you plan your future and decide where you and your company fit into the application matrix of the future.

I Am He As You Are He As You Are Me and We Are All Together

John Lennon, had he lived, probably would have loved the variations and possibilities of the Internet. But even though his song "I Am the Walrus" isn't about on-line identity, his phraseology goes a long way to address the issues that users and hosts face in determining if you are who you say you are and who that is, really.

For some, it's an e-commerce question, involving security issues, password-accessible account information and even smart card applications that protect and defend our own vital statistics. The continued rise in e-commerce and on-line purchases will require greater security measures including algorithm-protected smart card coding, discussed elsewhere in this book. However sophisticated our systems become, hackers will not give up the fight. Security on-line, like security anywhere else, will continue to be a key struggle.

A more esoteric struggle perhaps, will be with our own identities, something that doesn't relate to e-commerce at all. The Web's anonymity enables a wide variety of personal characteristics to emerge, not the least of which is based on the identity of the Web itself. If we're not who we say we are—or even if we choose to be honest and are who we say we are—we're still a mere atom in the Web's growing helical structure, enhancing its identity as we seek to use its strengths to enhance our own.

It's the cyborg concept again, and this time it has even more of an impact thanks to the Web's ability to empower and promote interactivity. With the Web at our disposal, we can become more than who we say we are. By that same token, our involvement helps the Web grow in the same fashion. Identifying which of the two is the host organism, however, is a little more difficult.

Se Habla Esperanto?

By 2005, experts estimate that the Internet population worldwide will total more than 345 million. For nearly half that number, English will not be the first language of choice. In fact, it may not be an option at all. If you want to continue to capitalize on the on-line market, or even just compete successfully on a global scale, your Web site better have multiple languages and multicultural capabilities. Otherwise plan to limit your commerce to markets significantly smaller than worldwide in nature.

Language translation is the first thing that comes to mind. Industry watchers already predict that the translation services and software business will grow from roughly $11 billion to more than $20 billion by 2004. But there's more to it than being able to describe your widgets as coming in *rojo*, *blanco* and *azul*. Your enterprise also must function in ways appropriate to both the business and culture of the countries you serve. This requires sensitivity to taxes, prices, import and export laws and restrictions, privacy and any other rules of doing business abroad. Your workflow, too, must be sensitive to their needs and desires first, and your operational obligations second. Blending that with your own corporate policies and goals will be the challenge of the new century.

While business is one thing, culture is quite another. Your Web site and business profile must be sensitive to the colors, symbols, folkways and mores that mean something to the purchasing population. We all know the story of how the Chevrolet Nova failed in Latin America because it's name, in Spanish, means "doesn't run." There are elements far more insidious than language that could undermine your Web efforts as the Internet tries to fill the role of on-line ambassador for your business. Learn them now so they won't come back to haunt you later.

The Whole World in His/Her Hand

Computers began as room-sized, then shrunk to desktop- and laptop-sized and now have become palm-sized. Will a microchip-powered secret decoder ring be next? The bounds may be limitless, but the trend is clear. As capability and capacity increase, size and limitations decrease. These days, it's all about wireless. Mobile technologies have become the darlings of the marketplace. That trend will continue with even greater emphasis as applications spread throughout industries and operational levels. Executives and staff at all levels will need to tap into the company database no matter where they are, and where they are will be less likely to be at their desks and in their offices than ever before. It won't just be cellular phones anymore, either. Personal devices will take on a whole new set of characteristics and capabilities.

Supporting systems will need to grow right along with those applications. Mobile technologies such as wireless application protocol (WAP), wireless area networks (WANs) and short message services (SMS) will be the wave of the present, with new applications just around the corner in a rapidly approaching future. In an industry riddled with acronyms, you will see letter combinations you never thought of representing applications and processes you've thus far seen only in your dreams. Wireless options will continue making more of those dreams into reality.

Helping fuel that desire will be greater dependence on on-line education, at the elementary, secondary and professional level. The same need for increased mobility exists, meaning the next generation—or maybe even this one—will access its lessons not from their classroom desks, but from somewhere in the field. Even the armed forces will enter this arena, and when they operate in the field, demands for accessibility, flexibility and durability increase significantly.

Up Close and Personal

We have already discussed the explosive growth in Web access. We noted its pervasive influence on our lives, both personal and business. We even discussed its increasing ease of use, immediacy and intimacy for users. All of this will grow as more and more market segmenting and niching takes place and as companies and merchants seek to get beyond your eyes and into your wallets, electronic or otherwise.

Thanks to new software programs, the Web and especially e-commerce will try to get up close and personal with you through increased personalization and content management designed to make you think you're the only person who's tuned into the Internet at that moment. This may even get to the point of human involvement to answer questions that you may have in real time and field on-line chat experiences designed to build a bond between you, the company, the Web site and the product. In a high-tech world such as this, warm and fuzzy may be the only competitive strategy left.

Five Trends to Watch

Predicting the on-line future is fortune-telling at its finest. However, some things stand out in their dominance. Here are five facets that are currently under discussion or soon will be in the vastly changing on-line world:

- *My kingdom for more bandwidth!* New programs and services and increased customer traffic usually mean a greater demand for capacity. Some already call it the World Wide Wait as they struggle to get on-line. Any methodology that can unclog this info-jam and provide more of the necessary bandwidth, channels or other options will be welcomed with open arms. That goes for the Web itself as well. Will the day come when we have four Webs, just like we have four television networks (more if you count cable)? Maybe. Something somewhere is going to have to give.

- *Taxation of Internet representation.* Members of the World Wide Web Consortium may want the Internet to retain its free, noncommercial status just like the public airwaves. But the day is coming when governments everywhere are going to crack down on the sales taxes they've been missing for the past decade. It's all about revenue and who's to say that the Information Superhighway won't become a toll road as a way to offset this otherwise free ride?

- *How crowded can it get?* Whether you're on the user side or the vendor side, cruising the Web is about as much fun as trying to merge on to the interstate during rush hour. For vendors, there are too many people with too few skills and too little interest in buying. For users, there are too many people selling and not enough sharing. As for the objectivity and capability of search engines...well, with banner ads and corporate sponsors, everyone is suspect these days. We alluded to it earlier but there's a shakeout coming that will attempt to make sense of the resources and untangle the knots and messes that currently hamstring the Web.

- *The Privacy Question.* Other industries, such as financial services, have had to deal with it for years. When to comes to the Internet, however, the stakes are raised significantly. How do we retain our rights and our vital information as private citizens if everyone we've dealt with does business on-line and has access to our records? Big Brother is not only watching, he's running analyses of our net worth, examining our buying habits and patterns, and studying our family's behavior and demographics. And we don't like that.

- *The Rise of Cyber Crime.* Does a week go by when someone doesn't unleash a new virus designed to terrorize the on-line neighborhood? Is there a government agency or large corporation whose database hasn't been hacked and vital records lost, stolen or altered? The Web is an unguarded highway and there are bandits at every bend in the road. And that's not even counting the increasing threat to companies' well-being from insiders bent on theft or embezzlement. Investigating and prosecuting cyber crimes is increasingly difficult, but the need for it becomes more prevalent every day.

When all is said and done, the net result is strategic turmoil on-line. Companies attempting to identify the right direction will have to find their own way, often without the aid of laws, rules or even guidelines. The optimists among us might call it a brave new world. For others, it's just another form of chaos.

The Cyborg Cometh. And Cometh.

Whether we're talking from a personal or professional perspective, the answer is roughly the same: Unlike any other media, the Internet offers extensions and opportunities that take us to new worlds, not only overseas and around the globe but to new levels of understanding within ourselves. Chaos often rules because it can—interaction means increased creativity and a rulebook as variable as the individuals interacting on-line. Rampant diversity changes the

Web's opinion and direction hundreds of times each day. Dialogues are interruptible, disposable and self-contradictory. Each person who logs on is the boss of his or her own world, the leader of his or her own enterprise, the alpha male or female of his or her own pack.

Can we survive with such a high level of disorder? It's up to all of us to find a way. And the best or worst part of this equation is that we're only just beginning.

Appendix SA
How to Find and Retain Good IS People

Achieving World-Class Results Requires World-Class People

You do not need an entire staff of world-class employees to achieve success, but you certainly do need some. The achievement capability level of your best people determines your theoretical upper limit of success. Realistically, however, you will likely achieve far less than that theoretical level.

Do not be misled by the fact that a well-organized and motivated group of level-B people will easily outperform a disorganized and unmotivated group of level-A people. Just remember that a well-organized and motivated group of level-A people will outperform a well-organized and motivated group of level-B people.

All of this is intended to encourage you to put your most intense and concentrated efforts into getting world-class people to work for you. You want to find people who are better than you. You may have become an IS manager because you have consistently been highly skilled. But to build on that, you must attract (and keep) IS people who are better than you are. You want to attract and keep IS people who are better than anybody.

As an IS manager, or any manager for that matter, you often do not have total control over such issues as salary. The corporation will dictate a specific budget to you, and you must work within those parameters. However, there are other non-advertised ways to get extra money for salary offers in your organization. There are some very savvy, not to say crafty, people in the organization who know these secrets. They may or may not be in human resources but you have to identify them, get them to like you or at least respect you, and then very patiently wait until they decide to help you on special occasions. Money is limited—use it wisely. Special favors are limited—use them wisely.

So how do you find these world-class people? Advertise. Talk to the marketing people. They know the principles, they know the level of effort required, and they know how to compare the cost of advertising to the return on investment. You must figure out what it is worth, in advertising dollars, to get a higher-level LAN administrator, programmer, or Web designer.

Talk to the IS people working for you and see if they know anyone who is highly skilled, shares the vision of the corporation and the department, and might be interested in a challenging job. If you can create a sense of excitement, challenge, and mutual care among your staff, they might be motivated to attract their friends and colleagues to your organization.

Mix consultants in with your employees. Consulting firms are good at attracting talented IS people who are experienced and often fairly good teachers as well. It is important that you make it clear that you will only accept very competent people. You should have no qualms whatsoever about rejecting people who do not hit the ground running and work well with your people. Keep your relationship with the consulting firm very friendly, but be ready to reject three or four consultants for every one you keep.

Interviewing the Technical Employee

If you have not had extensive interviewing experience, there are some basics you should know. For instance, you may be subconsciously influenced by how the prospective employees cut their hair, how they are dressed, and how firmly they shake your hand when they look you in the eye. You may not be prepared for these responses, but you need to know how powerfully they may affect you. And you need to understand that physical appearance and bearing may have no reflection at all on a person's knowledge and capabilities.

You will also be influenced by how well prospective employees respond during the interview. People who answer your questions with one word might frustrate you, but IS people who can solve a complex problem with few words are invaluable. Applicants who are good at interviews will expand on answers with examples of their experience, and will tell you things about their approach to dealing with problems. It will be much easier and more enjoyable to interview them. But the important thing to remember is that you are not so much hiring a person who is a good interviewee as much as a skilled computer technician. It doesn't hurt if they are good at interviews, but do not let communication skills lead you to select better interviewers over better employees.

Ask questions that lead the applicants to reveal what they know, what they have done, and who they are. Do not ask your mail administrator applicants, "Have you had much experience with Microsoft Outlook, or GroupWise, etc.?" Instead, ask them, "How would you design a mail system that works well for the users and doesn't fail too often?" If experience in the specific mail system is very important to you, add a second question after they have answered the first question, such as, "How would that be done in Outlook/GroupWise etc.?"

Give more weight in your evaluations to strong character, self-initiative, good practices, and extensive general experience than to specific experience with the product you use. Specific experience is often very important, but it is easier to learn Oracle than to learn to be creative and dependable. Make that a distinguishing principle for close calls. Just do not get too carried away with your opinion of how good you are at predicting character from an interview.

Once you sense that the person you are interviewing is the person you need for the job, roles will immediately switch. You become the applicant and the applicant becomes the interviewer. Recognize that moment and give your prospective new employee a sense of your vision for what the organization can accomplish and how he or she will become a key part of that vision. If you know how to give employees responsibility and interesting challenges, tell them how you will do that. The most important thing you can do to attract world-class people is to give them a sense of the vision and importance they will be part of when they join your organization.

Retaining Skilled Employees

You keep employees by paying them roughly the going market rate and by providing a good place to work. Be on the alert for frustration indicators such as too much stress in some people and boredom in others. People who are bored with their work perform poorly and often spend time dreaming about another job. Fortunately, the information technology field provides tremendous opportunities to avoid boredom. Just do not get lax in your job as a manager and fail to see when people are getting trapped in repetitive work.

If you follow the management principles listed here you will give people a lot of independence and responsibility. You will avoid telling them what to do. Instead, tell them what needs to be accomplished and let them figure out what needs to be done to accomplish the goals.

Everyone seems to agree that IS people love to learn new things. A lot of that is achieved by being aggressive in your adoption of new technologies. I recognize the benefits of being slightly behind the early adopters of new technologies. Just be aware that if you consistently lag too far behind new technologies, the really creative and effective people will begin to drift off into jobs with other companies. You do not have to entertain them by letting them play with every new toy that comes along, but you absolutely have to challenge the technical abilities of your best people. The best people are usually four or five times more efficient and effective than the second-best people. Do not let them get bored.

Training poses an extremely difficult problem. The money is tough, of course; almost all good courses are expensive. Computer-based training is becoming more effective but is still also expensive and will always be six months to a year behind good classroom training. Aside from the money, though, it is very difficult to find time to send the best people to training. It is far easier to send the less critical people to class; so they get most of the training. Of course, they need the training to improve, but your best people will return much more return on your investment dollar. Creative people will become more valuable to you through their interface with other people in training classes. They love to learn. That is how they got as good as they are. It can hurt your current project to let your stars go to training, and you may be criticized—but do it anyway.

Flexibility is key to keeping your employees happy. Be very, very flexible about letting people take care of their families. Make them feel comfortable about taking time off with no prior notification. People have jobs because they want to take care of their families. Set an example of diligence and hard work. Work plenty of long hours yourself. That way they know the flexibility for their family is out of concern for them and that the usual way is dedication and hard work. Do not give them the impression that it is unimportant that they take time for sick children or that their family concerns are a low priority.

In Conclusion

People love to succeed in important tasks, they love to be challenged, they love to get paid, and they appreciate concern for their families and personal needs. Give your people all the independence and responsibility you can offer. Then work on how to get braver so you can give them more. If they fail, it is natural to feel disappointed. Let them know that you are disappointed in the results but that you trust them. Then figure out together how they will succeed next time. Then really shock them by giving them even more responsibility in the same area.

Appendix SB
Implementing an Internet Project

How to Deploy Web Technology in an Organization

It is likely that you have already started implementation of Web technology in your organization. You may have a Web site and are now thinking seriously of what e-commerce might mean for your company. Following are some suggestions for how to take that technology to the next level.

There are stages that most organizations must go through to integrate Web technology into the culture of the organization. These are not just stages that the IS department has to go through—they are just the catalysts, the initial providers of infrastructure. Understanding the tools and the ways in which they might be used to benefit the core mission is a must for the rest of the company as well.

The first step in changing the way you do business using Web technology is the part you have probably already begun—getting people familiar with the Internet. You probably have an Internet site already, but is the care and feeding of the Internet solely an IS responsibility or has it moved into the corporate culture?

The best way to move Internet technology into the corporate culture is to ensure that the businesspeople (i.e., non-IS staff) understand and use it. In addition, the businesspeople should also be the content providers to the Web site. Read that again and believe it—do not allow your IS people to put the content onto the Web site. The site may be designed by the IS staff, but once it is in place the businesspeople must have the tools enabling them to put content directly on the Web site.

At the inception of a new corporate Web site, IS staff members must introduce Web concepts and tools to the rest of the organization. Some departments of the organization will likely have staff members who are already experts in Web technology. This knowledge should be encouraged. Allow them to expand this knowledge as quickly as they can. Then the IS staff can instruct the rest of the staff who may be afraid of technology or who are slow in adopting it. The IS department often wants to maintain standards and take ownership of the Web. It is important to have good tools and consistent rules in place; however, they may need to be sacrificed for speed and breadth of adoption by non-IS people in the early stages. This is a race where the fastest will win, and the most organized will only get honorable mention.

Although your IS staff will prefer powerful and more complex Web tools, businesspeople should be given simple tools that they can be successful with quickly. When they outgrow the simple tools, you can provide them with something more advanced. The IS staff should not be a bottleneck preventing a businessperson from putting useful information directly onto the Web site— and the reverse is true as well. When the IS staff trains groups in how to put information on the Web, those groups will want their newly trained Web people to take information from everyone else in the company and put it on the site themselves. This should also not be allowed to happen.

The way to transform an organization and move forward on the Internet is by having the first responsible source of information put the information directly onto the Web. Any approval processes should be discouraged. Staff members should be responsible for both the accuracy and the speed of posting. This can be a very difficult cultural transition. Most corporate systems are designed to avoid mistakes, and therefore typically contain slow approval processes. If mistakes are made in putting information on the Web, it is better to find out why and fix the process rather than slowing down all the other processes that are not introducing mistakes.

The key to the system is to clearly identify the person actually putting information on the particular page. There should not be an organization, nor a committee, nor an office symbol listed as the content provider—just a real human being with a name, an e-mail address, and a phone number. This provider should be the person who is the most reliable source for the information. Instant feedback is the most effective teacher, creating a one-to-one correspondence between data and provider—instantly adjustable information provided by an instantly accessible author. This is the magic of the Internet.

Introducing an Intranet Site

An Internet site is generally regarded as a source of information for people outside of an organization. After your organization understands the care and feeding of an Internet site, it is time to introduce the intranet site. An intranet site is a site for internal use designed to improve the flow of information within an organization. Because actual work will be accomplished on this site, it will probably house complex applications.

The intranet site will also house information designed to be seen by insiders only. Security becomes very important here. The security on an Internet site is designed to prevent unauthorized changes. Security on an intranet site is needed to guard against bogus input as well as unauthorized viewing. After both an Internet and an intranet site have been established, it is imperative to make it clear to your organization exactly which information is appropriate for each site. That distinction will become extremely critical when you move to the third stage—the extranet.

Your first Internet site was probably just bare advertising. Your first intranet site will probably be the Web version of a bulletin board. People will begin posting all sorts of notices and updates. After a short time people may no longer look at the sites because they are not updated regularly or they contain useless information. Usage can be measured by putting a Web counter on every relevant page. When pages are no longer used, make that information widely known and understood. Force people to rethink the information that goes on the intranet and to improve the value of what is put up there.

Sooner or later, to improve the value of the information, more complex Web applications will have to be provided. The vast majority of the information will not come from people typing information onto the Web page. The information will be automatically updated in real time by a wide variety of databases and other automated sources. Think about creating a system in which someone can highlight a portion of an e-mail and drag it directly onto the Web site. E-mail is often the first source of new information within an organization. Make the transfer of that information to the Web fast, accurate, and easy.

Here is a hint for how to introduce new technology across an organization: Teach the administrative assistants first. Administrative assistants are often quick learners and usually have a good sense of the usefulness of new communications tools. They also understand the organization and its needs in a broader sense than many other people because of their daily contacts. When people complain about how hard the new technology is to learn, tell them who is already using it. Tell them to ask the administrative assistants for help, they have been using it for a while.

Taking It a Step Further—Extranets

After a while you will have developed a broad system of useful tools and information on your intranet. Some of this information would be extremely helpful to people outside of your organization. The resource used to provide outsiders access to your intranet is called an extranet. The potential for increased efficiency is enormous; however, the potential for security problems is also enormous.

How can you provide some of the information to outsiders without compromising the security of your internal site? The answer is your directory. A powerful and well-tested directory will allow you to very precisely control access to information on your intranet. You can control by name or group exactly who can access information on your intranet and precisely which bits of information they can see.

For example, Company A might be able to view your entire hardware inventory by week over the last three years. Maybe they are your hardware supplier and you want them to anticipate when you need a new shipment and prepare for it rather than waiting for you to ask. Company B might be able to view your plans for a new office layout. You can control by company, by group and by individual exactly who can see, or modify, any information on your site.

Once the employees in your company understand this and get good at it, they will be able to invent entirely new ways of doing their jobs. The potential for increased efficiency and effectiveness in your company can explode. Show your IS people the vision of where you can go. Let them take over and get you there at Internet speeds. You must inform your boss of your plans so you can obtain financial resources and also explain the flurry of activity. With support from both senior management and staff alike, the sky is the limit in what you can accomplish.

Appendix SC
Security Revisited

Security is a dynamic issue. For every new defense, a new offense seems to form. The Melissa virus of 1999 ripped through e-mail systems at many corporations. People were not well educated on the rule that you don't open executable files in e-mail that you didn't request. The denial of service attacks on the Internet in early 2000 also illustrated an attack that quickly overwhelmed defenses. In this case, the affected sites were able to stop future attacks quickly. Credit was given to an existing reaction plan for such problems.

In another publicized account, someone broke into an e-commerce site and stole thousands of credit card numbers. The affected company did the prudent thing and canceled all of the cards. However, imagine the customer satisfaction in learning that your credit card was just canceled because of a mistake someone else made. Therefore, as IS manager, your job of preserving security has increased a notch with each new year.

The Layered Approach

In a perfect world you would have all day to work on security issues and stay up to date on threats. Unfortunately, you are already working 12-hour days fighting off dozens of different problems and attempting to keep your management team happy. Therefore, security tends to be addressed once in a corporation and then left alone for a very long time. This is the recipe for disaster.

Instead, you need to regularly review the security issues, even appoint a permanent security manager. You also need to address security at several different levels. There is the issue of the physical security of the network, the software security of the network, risks from outside users of the network, and thorough management of the system. Let's examine each of these separately.

Physical Security

As mentioned in the main volume, you always begin a discussion of security with a list of the potential threats to your system. To this we need to add a complete description of the system to be protected, especially where it begins and ends. At these points you will need to look at what level of protection is available outside of your system. The best way to crack a computer system is to get inside a company.

Therefore, you examine the overall security procedures at your company. If people are free to wander around the building without challenge or limit to access, a tight computer security system is required. If outside vendors can log into computers at the company that are connected to your network in any way, you have a major vulnerability to be addressed. If terminals connected to the Internet are not logged off when not in use, you have another major issue.

Thus, you need to tie down the physical security of your system by making sure that all network-related machinery is safe from fire, water, wind, dust, theft, and the like. The servers, routers, and switches of your system must be in locked areas with limited access. For example, the hub that controls the LAN in my office is out in the open. I plugged my laptop into the hub using a two-foot CAT5 cable and quickly gained unchallenged access to my network. An outsider could have copied all accessible data files and walked away.

We will also repeat the golden rule of computers—always have a backup. That means all data must be backed up and stored in a separate and safe location. For example, if you run a Web server performing e-commerce, you should be running a mirror backup to a separate server. The Internet connection should be serviced by software that can instantly switch connections to the backup machine if the dedicated cable or your ISP suffers an outage.

In our situation, we co-locate our Web servers at an ISP with extremely wide bandwidth. A dedicated and secured data line passes backup data to our office server. The ISP already has backup communication protection and daily data backup procedures. Our copy of the data comes in hourly and we are ready to re-route traffic to our machine in an emergency.

The Software Layer

The largest problem for security has been at the software level. Most of the Internet-related security disasters have been the result of hackers taking advantage of weaknesses in the software. Take the example of a company that installs a Windows 2000 server package and then hooks up a Web site using IIS. The IS manager in this example is betting his or her job on the security of off-the-shelf products and nothing else.

What needs to be done is an installation of the latest software patches for the system. Therefore, you must constantly monitor your vendors for updated information on discovered security problems. The patches must be installed and updated as needed. Specific corrections to the system must always be taken. Most problems will result from neglecting a patch or upgrade.

Take the example of buffer overflow. In some programming languages you can enter information into a field that includes programming commands that the Web site will dutifully execute. This flaw in several languages and protocols has been used to open access to systems or to overwhelm the site and bring it down. Worse still is that a well-educated attacker can gain access to hundreds of computer systems, install a Trojan horse program, and have all of these systems attack a specific site. That would make your company an unwilling participant in an attack. If the victim is one of your vendors or customers the political fallout could be tremendous.

What is required at the software level is protection at the points of attack. Today that means the physical crossing points in your system, servers, routers, and switches. Any place where IP packets get sorted out, exchanged, or distributed is a key target for attacks. Therefore, each of these points must have its own form of protections. Let's review some of the possibilities for each point.

Point of Connection

At one or more places in your system you have a connection to the Internet. This is always the first place to install security measures. With dedicated data lines you can place a firewall system or computer with the router attached to the dedicated line. The router and the firewall systems can be set for the level of defense your site requires. (Remember, the type of site you run will determine your level of risk. Government sites, e-commerce sites, portals, or controversial companies are high on the attack list.)

A good firewall will perform two important functions. One is to filter out unwanted IP addresses and the other is to audit people probing your system. In some cases you can set a dynamic IP address for your router with a command to only let through validated packets from your ISP. This makes it hard for attackers to find and dwell on your router looking for a hole. A typical attack on a router is someone's script asking for permission from the various ports (e.g., port 25 for your incoming mail service).

The auditing program should be set to detect any multiple requests in a very short period of time. The probe of ports is a test to see if you left any "doors open." If such a probe is detected, your security software should sound an alarm and record the origin of the probe. Working with your ISP, you have an outside chance of chasing down the culprit. However, it is very difficult to find most attackers, much less prove they are violating the law. Therefore, the strategy is to find the source of the attack and shut it off as far from your router as possible. If the ISP shuts off this account and IP address, the attacker has to falsify a new account and still doesn't know which intended victim detected the presence. With enough discouragement an attacker will look for easier pickings.

Another good step at the firewall level is to translate IP addresses. All incoming IP packages are addressed to the firewall. Once approved, a software routine re-addresses them to the correct computer within your system. Packets coming out of your system are retranslated to the firewall's IP address. All outsiders see is the firewall's address. They cannot "see" your internal IP addresses. If they could they would be able to piece together your addressing system and exploit your system.

Finally, you need to look for remote access capabilities on your routers and other equipment. Shut as many of these off as possible. A router with a capability to be reprogrammed remotely is a liability when not properly configured. Reprogramming of routers should only take place at the router or from a secure computer using a single, validated IP address. Again, you should set auditing software to monitor these features for tampering.

Switches

Switching hardware is a victim of attacks because switches are usually left defenseless. When connecting together several LANs, the switches are commonly left open to all traffic. Thus, an attacker can gain access to one LAN and gather log-ins and passwords for users on the connected LANs. Therefore, you want to limit traffic through the switches to authorized users only.

Servers

Once an attacker successfully enters a server, a world of potentially damaging information is available. Everything from passwords to credit card files can be obtained. Thus, the highest level of security is typically centered on the servers. This begins by limiting the capabilities of each server. For example, an e-mail server should have all nonrelated functions shut off. Unused ports that are left open are like unlocked doors to a building.

At the audit level, you should establish an alarm whenever anyone tries to access a port that has been turned off. At the same time you need packet filters in strategic positions within your system to ensure that traffic is coming from valid locations. For example, an Internet-based packet that is carrying the identification of an internal IP address is suspicious. The packet should be stopped and the audit trail started.

Encryption is strongly encouraged for sites serious about security. Encryption of messages, databases, and command codes is a minimum. Services like SSL only protect the messages passing back and forth on the Internet. The collected data on your server can still be unencrypted. Or, try this experiment. Next time you need a password to log into a Web site, look at the URL box and see if your password is being clearly displayed in the requested address. This is all an attacker needs to see to gain access.

Now, to pull all of this off you need to be consistent and diligent. Be consistent in conducting at least monthly audits of the error logs and security logs of your servers and other systems. Look for things like unauthorized access attempts, normally sound programs returning odd error messages, multiple password attempts, and the like. This is evidence of an attacker working on your system.

Being diligent means that you are thorough in setting up your security system. In larger systems this can be quite a headache. You need to know which groups need access to which services. Once the pattern for these is established, you then must go through the entire setup again to look for weak points. This requires you to think like an attacker. You need to look for holes in your security system and plug as many as possible. Then you have to test the entire system to make sure that everyone granted permission for access is indeed getting the proper access. It never goes smoothly, so you repeat this cycle a few times and only make compromises as infrequently as possible.

If you are really serious about security, you live the hacker's life. Typically you appoint someone on staff to make weekly visits to the discussion sites for hackers. Learn how they think, what they like to target, and the tricks they learn. Use this knowledge to look at your own system. The weaknesses in systems will be discussed at these sites first, long before a security patch will be available for your system.

You will also want to stay tuned to the security sites that have daily updates on problems detected in the Internet world. For example:

- *www.cert.org*—Has a wonderful update service, newsletter, and white papers on security issues.
- *www.interhack.net*—Discusses a variety of security topics.
- *comp.risks*—Is a newsgroup dedicated to discussing security risks.

Search engine searches on keywords such as "Internet security," "firewall," and "hackers" will lead you to other interesting sites. However, be very careful when downloading any software from these sites as they are typically under attack themselves by people trying to be more clever than the experts.

Strategies and Tactics

Let's take some specific concerns about security and discuss the strategies and tactics that would be used to counteract the threats. For example, let's start with a common threat—viruses arriving through e-mail.

The overall strategy would be to prevent any virus from getting into your system from the e-mail server. The key feature is that no virus gets into your e-mail service without detection. The greatest danger is that a virus would arrive into your system undetected. It would then have the capability of replicating itself into other parts of your Internet system before the detection would occur from service failures or other symptoms.

On a tactical level, this strategy needs to be implemented by selecting specific locations, times, and situations that need to be addressed with specific countermeasures. Let's look at locations and see how our tactical approach is applied.

1. *The users.* The end users of your Internet system are probably mixed in with the users of the local area network. Therefore, there is first and foremost a great need for training and awareness for the employees. They need to realize that they are one of the monitoring systems you depend upon to report possible virus attacks. For example, they must be trained to not open file attachments on their e-mails that they did not request. This is a particularly tricky situation because e-mail can carry copies to other recipients bearing the name of someone from your company. Assuming that it came from an internal source, most people will open the infected file without thinking twice. Your job is to make these people think twice.

2. *The e-mail reader.* Each computer attached to the Internet or an Internet service will usually have a program for collecting and reading e-mail. Modern virus detection software can work with these programs to scan for infected files. For example, in McAfee VirusScan you can set up the V-Shield portion of the program to actively scan each e-mail attachment for viruses. However, this has to be done manually for each machine. At the same time, this does not give you 100 percent protection, but it will provide many cases of early warning of a virus arriving at your company. From that point you need to have a reaction plan for how you will notify the users to watch out for the attack, as well as how you plan to search and clean the system.

3. *The e-mail server.* E-mail will be received at a server within your company. This is where you should concentrate your antivirus systems. This includes virus scanning software, audit trails, activity monitors, and other software solutions that could alert you to either an attack or a probe before an attack. At the same time, you need to carry out firewall protection of this server because it represents one of the gateways into your protected community.

4. *The ISP.* Your provider of Internet services should also be working to prevent a virus attack. This will include scanning for viruses on their internal network and the scanning of the Internet flow for problems. Someone at your company should also be on the alert for pending attacks. Monitoring of hacker sites and the daily computer press is encouraged. If your company is about to launch a controversial product or if a major political problem encourages attacks on your type of company, you need to have a plan for how you will beef up security.

5. *Management.* Finally, you, as IS manager, and other members of the management team must be an active part of the protection plan. Policies have to be in place to make sure that an internal employee does not feed a virus deliberately into your system. This would include publicizing the legal consequences of such an action and the strength of your system in tracking down such a malicious employee.

In addition to these types of standard procedures for addressing security needs for particular locations, you can also practice some unconventional methods. For example, deception technology can be deployed. Take the example of an employee detecting a virus from the outside. Although it is nearly impossible to track down the source, you release a brief e-mail hinting that the person was found and in being prosecuted but not to mention this outside the company. The result is that internal employees believe that your system is even stronger than you indicated and are dissuaded from attempting a similar attack.

The Spam Threat

A major threat to security that is nearly impossible to stop is spam e-mail. Although most companies do not see it as a security threat, in reality it is a substantial threat. The damage is done in the time, bandwidth, disk space, and productivity lost to spam. Let's look at a specific example, a vacation getaway offer that arrives by fax and e-mail to a few users in your company.

If the fax was printed out on paper, then fax time and paper were wasted. Worse still is the case where an employee makes dozens of copies and starts passing them around. More time and paper are wasted. If an e-mail arrives with the same offer and is 8 KB in size, each copy made wastes that much more disk space. For really busy e-mail systems, this can quickly add up to the mailboxes at a desktop computer getting so large it slows down the entire operating system.

Therefore, you need to look at similar locations as the virus threat to reduce spam as much as possible.

1. *The users.* Again, there is a need to educate the users on the threat spam e-mail poses to productivity. Stopping to read through half a dozen worthless e-mails can burn 5 to 10 minutes of time each day. Multiply that by

the number of employees in the company and the days worked per year and you are wasting some serious time. Education will teach employees to skip over the obvious "junk" messages.

2. *The e-mail system.* Luckily there are now several software products available that allow you to screen out e-mail by keyword and sender. This will not stop all of the messages, but it will cut them down. For example, keywords such as "lottery," "hot girls," and the like can screen out some of the more obvious problems. However, these have to be used with care. Take our vacation offer above. If we screened out the word "vacation," employees e-mailing in vacation requests from home may find that the message never arrives. Therefore, the better approach is to mark the sources of spam e-mail by the origin address and screen them out. This prevents both current and future messages from that location.

3. *Management.* Believe it or not, there is a law against sending unsolicited faxes (Title 47, Chapter 5, Subchapter II). As a standard management procedure, we have a copy of the law with the portion on faxing highlighted stationed at every fax machine. A message on a fax form tells the sender to please remove us from their bulk fax list. This is sent in response to any junk fax. It is typically effective.

Naturally, you balance your attack on spam e-mail in proportion to the threat. This is not your highest priority, but it does deserve some time each month to cut down its volume.

New Sources of Attack and New Holes in Your System

At least a couple of times each year, you should stand back and look at your complete security system. Security threats are dynamic and changing. The first problem is that people are constantly finding new ways to defeat security systems or cause problems for Internet users. The second problem is that new services and features sometimes mean new openings into your computer system. Let's take a closer look at these two problems.

First, a new service like DSL or cable modems means that you have a new gateway into your network. Hooking an unprotected DSL line to a network-based computer means that outsiders now have an unprotected gateway into your system. This is a problem we have already addressed. Now think about the growing use of wireless connections to the Internet. Literally hundreds of employees could be in the field using their Palm Pilots and pocket PC devices to download infected files. Once back in the office they cradle their devices to synchronize with their desktop computer. One unprotected machine and you have a virus loose in your system.

Again, education and the proper deployment of antivirus software provide a good start to preventing this problem. Employees should be made aware of the threat of downloading files from untrusted sources. At the same time, files being transferred into a computer from the USB or serial ports should be scanned.

Now, think about an even larger problem—the employee's Palm Pilot is stolen at the airport. On the system are the log-in name and password for accessing your network's e-mail system. Now the thief has a valuable piece of information. The access can be sold to a competing company that can open and read confidential e-mail. Or the thief can do this and sell important information to competitors or release product information to the press.

Preventing this situation is even harder because the employee can go for one or more days before discovering the loss. In our office, all laptops and handheld devices are not allowed to store passwords. It is up to the employee to enter the password for access each time the device is used or an outside connection is requested. Then a thief will have a very difficult time trying to crack through the security. This buys the time we need for the employee to report the loss and let us change or shut down accounts.

The other problem for your security system is that new ways are always being found to get around existing security systems. One way to handle this is to be a moving target. New security configurations and updates can be added to your system at regular intervals. That way the openings in your system keep moving around or they shut suddenly. This makes outside attack more difficult.

Being aware of problems at other companies is a very good defense. When the first denial of service attacks occurred in 2000, smart companies promptly called either the affected company or their computer consultants to learn how the attack was carried out and what prevented future attacks. One of the companies brought under attack actually had predicted the possibility of such an attack. The network monitoring software sounded an alert when an unnatural number of "ping" commands suddenly appeared. They shut down the "ping" service and cut off the attack before it could bring down their system.

Point of Connection

Finally, let's take a look at one location in particular, the point of contact with the Internet. It cannot be emphasized too strongly that if your company decides to connect to the Internet, you need to make several determinations first:

- Why are we doing this?
- How will we connect?
- What do we hope to accomplish?
- What are the threats?
- How do we prevent security breaches?

Always start with the reason you want to connect. Specifically, what was it that prompted your company to want to hook to the Internet? Perhaps the company wanted to be able to send e-mail to remote locations. Maybe you wanted to establish a strong Internet presence. Then again, you could be setting up your Enterprise Resource Planning (ERP) using the Internet, including electronic payment.

Each of these three example situations involves tremendously different levels of exposure and complexity. For each situation you must respond with an appropriate level of planning. A well-designed plan will account for your security needs and the strength of your system.

The next issue is how you will be connected. We have already talked about the issues surrounding the type of connections (i.e., DSL, T1, cable modem, etc.). What is to be addressed here is how that connection is made to your network. You can establish an independent network of computers to be used just for the Internet. A strong firewall between this network and the Internet is adequate in most situations. An intruder would not be able to get to your internal network. Management of the Internet system would include the banning of use or storage of sensitive information on the Internet dedicated computers.

However, most companies will need to have a link between machines dedicated for talking to the Internet and part or all of your internal network. In this case you will want to look into the usual firewall between the connections to the Internet and the routers. At the same time you want a really strong gateway system between the Internet computers and the rest of your internal network. Typically, a router would be used to send Internet-related traffic to either your Web servers or the internal network. A firewall would be put between that router and the internal network. Additional measures are also possible.

Next comes the question of how much you want to accomplish because you are hooked to the Internet. The company that only wants e-mail service would manually shut off Web, FTP, and other unrelated services. In addition, its presence on the Internet would be nearly invisible. Thus, many security measures would not be needed. In contrast, a company with a strong presence on the Internet needs to add a lot of security features to fend off attacks.

However, the security measures have to be designed so that the goals to be accomplished by the company are not restricted by the system. A company that wants a large sales force that can pick up price information from any location using the Internet will not be able to easily restrict IP addresses that are allowed into the system.

Naturally, you also take the time to look at the number and level of threats that are presented to the system. This should be a critical part of your planning process. If necessary, you can rank each threat by the likelihood that it will happen times the potential damage it could cause. This will allow you to prioritize the threats that absolutely have to be addressed versus the trivial threats.

Finally, there is the question of how to prevent a security breach, as opposed to reacting once a breach is detected. This is a management-level activity. Preventive action involves management reviewing the entire computer system. This is the process of collecting information about the system from many sources. This can include audit reports, incident reports, logbooks, interviews with operators, control charts, and the like.

From this, management must create a picture of what is possible in the way of security breaches within your system. As IS manager, you must supply a list of the various ways people can intrude on your system. For example, how do you know that the top managers' authorization keys for e-mail have not been copied? Working together, you look at potential threats and plan actions to prevent the threats from becoming a reality. In the case of a major e-commerce site, this can be a full-time job.

A Specific Example—Malicious HTML Tags

There are many examples of how security on the Internet can be compromised. Let's look at one specific example to see how it works and how you would work to prevent it from affecting your system.

A little-known trick with Web pages is that you can plant executable scripts within an HTML tag. A Web page that allows users to write out their own HTML message will also allow an intruder to plant a script in the message. The next user of the page will execute the script. This can pass viruses or other problems to users through Web page links, e-mail, or newsgroup postings.

This type of problem has to be attacked in several ways. First, you have to educate your personnel not to fill out HTML messages on other sites. This will involve educating them on the potential dangers. Second, you have to train people to be careful when exploring new newsgroups or untrusted Web sites. Web sites of suspicious nature should be blocked by your access control.

At the same time, you must have your virus detection software set at each workstation to alert you of a problem. Quickly checking the log and history files of the Web browser and other Internet software in use should allow you to pin down the source of the attack. In this way you can quickly shut off access to the accused site.

Also, having reaction plans in place will help you to control the damage done by any form of successful intrusion into your system. Management must work to ensure the problem won't occur again. The damage done must be repaired and the workforce educated to prevent a similar incident.

What Can an IS Manager Do?

This leads to the question we have been referring to throughout this chapter—how is an IS manager going to be able to keep up with a world of growing threats? The answer is to use his or her existing resources wisely by following a carefully laid out plan. The idea is to attack the problem at many different layers.

This means the development of an architecture of security. Too many companies put a firewall in place and call that the security system. This may be fine for a small office with half a dozen employees. However, any company of size or a company with valuable data products to protect needs defense in depth.

As we have stated earlier, the first level of defense is the physical security of your network. Make sure that servers, RAID arrays, data backup, and the like are behind locked doors with a security alarm in place. The best way to get data is to steal the actual computer.

The second level of defense comes at the routers, your first point of contact with the Internet. If possible, also get the ISP to defend their routers. Use packet filtering to keep out unwanted traffic. Turn off the services you don't use or want, such as ping, traceroute, and the like. You should deploy a system of setting up IP addresses on your internal network that are not allowed to be used for addressing messages to the outside Internet. This will deny the intruder the use of internal addressing to move around in your system or to imitate one of your users.

Next come the firewalls and packet filters used to keep out unauthorized traffic. What most IS managers forget to do is set the systems up to prevent attacks from being launched from within your system out to the Internet. This prevents a Trojan horse program from using your site to attack other sites. As attacks grow in number, the makers of firewalls get more clever in ways to block them. It is important to regularly update your firewall strategy to ensure that new forms of attack are denied.

Then you should design and place a proxy server on your system. This is a server that acts as an intermediary between your network and the Internet. It takes your network one step further away from the Internet. Only the proxy's address is available to the public. These should be paired with intrusion-detection systems. That way you can be alerted in real time to suspicious behavior coming from the Internet.

These are just some of the physical steps you can take. There also are the issues of education and trust. You need to educate the workforce on your security procedures and how they are to be used in daily Internet activities. This includes the prompt reporting of unusual activity at the desktop.

Trust is the process of establishing secured links between groups on the Internet. If you regularly depend on an outside Web site for information, you should look into establishing dedicated or trusted connections. This can be done in any one of several ways, including the use of encryption and permission codes. That way only authorized users from your site are able to communicate with the trusted site. The trusted site, in turn, is able to detect others trying to interfere with the connection.

There Is Hope

Despite the daunting task this seems to present, there is hope for the IS manager. Internet users are beginning to recognize the basic weakness of the "walled city" approach to security. A better model is to band together to present an area-wide defensive system. Several organizations are working to make this a reality.

One is the National Institute of Standards and Technologies (NIST) in the United States. They are working on several committees to establish a wider range of security options and practices. For example, they are working on Role-Based Access Control whereby software will be able to assign individuals access control based on the role they play in a project in real time. As responsibilities change, the security system changes to allow access to new information while closing off access to data related to completed tasks. The cost and complexity of security are greatly reduced with this model.

NIST also works on the IPsec Project, an effort to provide greater levels of authentication, integrity, and confidentiality at the IP layer of the Internet. This includes an updating of the current Internet Protocol. The goal is to secure the infrastructure of the Internet and thus deny attackers a free reign of travel through the system. One way to do this will be to provide a central security policy for the entire Internet or specific sections of the Internet.

You can obtain more information by visiting the NIST computer security home page at:

Csrc.nist.gov

Another good organization to join and monitor is the International Computer Security Association (ICSA). Their Web site is at:

ncsa.net

This site lists the newest forms of security attacks and how to prevent them. It also discusses security administration and other important topics. They also provide software and certification services.

Summary

Security is still the major concern for e-commerce sites. Through a proactive plan by management, a company can prevent many types of attacks from within and without. At the same time, your company must have security policies, a reaction plan for security problems, and a regular review of security threats. Only by being active and dynamic can you secure your IS manager's job by demonstrating your constant ability to prevent disaster.

Appendix SD
Keeping Up with Your Newfound Internet Responsibilities

So, you've been transferred to head of IS or suddenly your umbrella has been extended into looking over the Web folks down the hall. And you're a hard worker, a quick study, and a good manager. Honestly though, you aren't a geek, and you're faking your way through the technology parts. This happens all the time because there's a desperate need for technology workers who are good managers, but often one half of the equation is missing. Your job is to become "wired" by Monday. Well, the good news is that nobody is ever truly "caught-up" in the Internet universe, because the technology moves faster than humanly comprehensible. The real job is to be able to constantly learn, constantly expand, and constantly play catch-up. The cliche of "surfing" waves of information is an apt one.

The upside is that you can't get too far behind either, because data that's two years old is simply compost for the endlessly rising data pile. The skills required include sniffing out new ideas, stepping back to look at emerging trends, and being able to abstract complex information into clear and simple statements. These are the manager's technology requirements.

Getting Up to Speed—Great Sources

Over and over the best IS managers cite periodicals, magazines, and technology news sites as their sources for information. This works against the grain of corporate culture, however, because people who are sitting around reading are not considered to be "working." It probably means lots of magazine perusal after work and on weekends, but don't pretend that a half-hour at lunchtime is enough to keep in the flow of things. It's going to be a couple of hours a day for a while before you discover the magazines that are pertinent to you. Just go to a big bookstore and hit the computing section of the periodicals rack. Start browsing and don't stop until the place closes. Don't bother with the book section either—that's for focused reading when you know what you need precisely. The magazines are more like an environment to graze in; don't worry about any one bite, because what you want is a little taste of everything.

When you pick up a copy of *BYTE Magazine*, you're probably going to be rather daunted by the sheer volume of incomprehensible articles. It will stay that way for a while, but just remember that it's that way for everyone. Start skimming articles that pertain to your important subjects today. You need a new server? Go look at the hardware and RAID Array articles. Skim the margin boxes on Apache and Linux. You won't understand most of what you read; accept it and get used to it. Skip to another subject that interests you. Learn to skim.

Is Dreamweaver still king? What's the status of Mozilla? What *is* Mozilla? You'll start with almost no understanding of any subjects, but soon there will be cross-references. Pick up *Web Developer Magazine* and browse Java articles for information on the latest tools. You're not a Java coder, so just read articles that discuss client relations, or emerging ideas, or perhaps good interfaces. Don't plough too deeply into stuff you don't understand, just keep moving. Remember, there's lots of paper on that rack. Buy 10 different magazines, and remember to write it all off as a tax deduction. Expense it even, whatever you can get away with. Subscribe to those magazines, because if you don't you'll let the whole thing slip. Magazines should become a constant background buzz at your fingertips. Some people keep old issues, but they don't seem to go back to them, and old copy certainly isn't part of "media as current environment."

There is a general set of technology news sources that will prove to be an excellent starting point for you to gather technology information. For the most general information on a daily basis, try these sites:

http://www.sjmercurynews.com/svtech/
http://www.zdnet.com/anchordesk/

To pull even further back, turn to either:

http://www.fortune.com/fortune/

or

http://www.wired.com

It should come as no surprise that *Fortune* magazine has turned hard and fast into a new economy-focused magazine and Web site. Meanwhile, *Wired* magazine has moved into the mainstream to keep its place as the culture's "hip technology source" standard-bearer, though *Wired* is more focused on technology culture than on technology itself. For meatier daily news, and arguably the most referred to news source by the technically literate, check out www.slashdot.org for everything "geek" on the planet today. Slashdot is the most savvy of the news sites lately, and because of its popularity with system administrators around the world, Slashdot often has inside scoops direct from the source, sources that may even circumvent the public relations department. You usually hear it at Slashdot first, whether it's the Microsoft court case, Nanotech developments, or a leak of the latest Apple machine spec.

On the other hand, http://www.zdnet.com/eweek/ will provide a more focused stream of Internet information and lots of community resources to answer the seemingly unanswerable. If you want a great source of information on networking as a whole, check out http://nwfusion.experts-exchange.com/. If you need to keep up with Apple news, http://macworld.zdnet.com/ and the evangelical http://www.macaddict.com/ will prove excellent sources for OS X information. And Mac Addict always has the best articles on why Macintosh "should" take over the world, and a host of accompanying commentary explaining Bill Gates' nefarious plans to keep Apple down.

Making the Most of the Internet

There are two general purposes to the Internet, one of which I'll get to later in this appendix. The first goal is to provide pertinent information as fast as possible to the user. It isn't often met, and the hurdles will make you just want to dial 411, ask your secretary, call your mom, or go find a dictionary—anything to avoid using the Internet. It is a valid complaint. However, there are some general tool sites out there that will often ease and expedite the task at hand if you are willing to put in a little practice. The following selections are ones that I use on a day-to-day basis for any of a number of reasons. They are certainly personal preferences rather than a set of rigid endorsements.

For searches I have two main sites. When I know what I'm looking for, I go to http://www.google.com/. Google searches the widest spectrum of the Web and has a very clean interface. But http://hotbot.lycos.com/ is where I go when I don't know what I'm looking for, because Hotbot provides an array of subject headings and fields that will herd me into some niche of the Internet I never knew existed. This is pretty handy sometimes. If you want to know the search systems of tomorrow, go to http://bots.Internet.com/ and see what's going on with Bots. This site is filled with the latest and greatest on Bots. And although they haven't taken over the Internet today, wouldn't it be nice to be at least partially aware of a technology on the horizon? I use http://www.dictionary.com/ to find words, http://www.mapquest.com/ to find places, and http://www.smartpages.com/ to find people and businesses. I still keep a dictionary and a phone book handy, though; paper has its advantages.

When I want to buy a product on-line, I start at http://www.mysimon.com/, which has the nifty feature of trolling the Web for all instances of a product and listing them according to price (or several other criteria) with a vendor who is given a reliability rating. This, in turn, has usually led me to either http://www.onvia.com for its wide range of products, or http://www.outpost.com for great prices and fast delivery. Outpost.com also has the funniest commercials I've ever seen.

Before you buy anything, though, it is critical to review endlessly. The systems administrators will have opinions, so will the Web page designers, the secretaries, and so on. And if it pertains to their field, and you are a good manager, you will listen to them. You should also look on http://www.zdnet.com/, and http://www.zdnet.com/pcmag/ to see what the critics think. Ziff Davis owns most of the technology magazines both on- and off-line, and their database of product reviews is gargantuan. Product reviews are actually an excellent starting spot to learn about any technology subject from a manager's standpoint. What you need to know is not how to keep a server running, but what sorts of problems arise during the task. Is it a hardware, software, or user issue? When will there be problems because of high volume? What other tools are required? These are the issues getting tossed around by the techs, and you will at least be able to listen without a slack jaw if you have heard of the tools they use.

Site Building

If you've never coded or built a Web site, here is a project that will change your entire understanding of the Internet and how it really works and is used. This is the second goal of the Internet, which I referred to earlier. That goal is to allow an individual to change the Internet environment, to change the way it responds to you, and to change what the Internet is. You are going to build a Web site. It will take about six hours for the complete newbie.

To get into the swing of things, head over to http://hotwired.lycos.com/ and check up on the latest Digerati news and art. Although they certainly are rather full of themselves, Hotwired manages to be an entertaining source for the general fads, movements, and attitude of the Web development community. When you need breaks, go back to Hotwired and download fun cartoons. Get a pad and paper and make a very simple layout with two pages, one picture that separates a title, and a paragraph of text. Then put in two links at the bottom. Make one of the links go to your second page and make the other go to a site you like. My first link was to *The New York Times*. Don't even worry about centering yet, just let it all fall along the left margin. Your second page can be more of the same, or maybe put in two pictures, one of which is a link itself. Remember to put in a link back to your first page.

Next, go to http://angelfire.lycos.com/ where you can build a personal Web site for free without having any pop-up ads or intrusive code stuck onto your new site. Just sign up and start. The tutorials are excellent, and the available tools are not at all shabby for the price, which is free. The site at http://hotwired.lycos.com/webmonkey/ also has excellent tutorials for the uninitiated. You could even snag an excellent shareware HTML editor at http://www.ultraedit.com. On the other hand, you could write all your code in Notepad, which will impress anybody who doesn't know anything about coding. Another thing you might want to get is a File Transfer Protocol (FTP) program in order to put your pages up on a server. You could just use Angelfire's "in browser" FTP Utility, but going to find your own is a good exercise. Try CuteFTP or LeechFTP or whatever else you find. There are lots of tools and utilities out there that basically do the exact same thing.

Start with just any old pictures and text, and remember that nobody will ever see it but you. It won't be half as ugly as my first site, let me assure you. Your real task here will be to grab images and snippets from around the Web, and put in links to any site that strikes you. To fancy things up, go to http://hotwired.lycos.com/webmonkey/ for bits of code and more advice on how to set up a page. Webmonkey's "How-to Library" is an excellent place to find all things Web-related, from marketing to code to Web tool listings. The ultimate source for site building is http://www.w3.org/. The Web Consortium establishes "The Standard" for all Web code. Is your document well formed? Is that HTML readable by Explorer 5.0? The folks at www.W3C.org know.

The real trick to this project is learning how to gather information and tools on the Web and then putting them to use. The process is one that will not only help you get stuff done, it will help you understand what your team is doing when they work, and it will help you understand what clients are tripped up by when they are trying to glean information from your own site. You will develop preferences and habits as you begin to do things to the Web, instead of just being a passive observer. We intuitively know how to click links, scroll around, and browse. That's all just like watching TV or flipping through a newspaper. It is harder to do things to a monitor, because we never did things to our televisions beside change the channel. Remember that it is only mind-set and practice that hold you back, though; it really isn't about brainpower when you're working on this level. Once you have turned the Internet into a two-way street, you will start to change the way you organize information. You will think in terms of users and team members with their own pages, and you will look at those pages as flexible, dynamic sources of information.

Further Reference

For further reference, see the following sites:

> http://hotwired.lycos.com/
> http://hotwired.lycos.com/webmonkey/
> http://angelfire.lycos.com/
> http://www.w3.org/
> http://nwfusion.experts-exchange.com/

http://www.zdnet.com/anchordesk/
http://www.slashdot.org
http://www.wired.com
http://www.fortune.com/fortune/
http://www.sjmercurynews.com/svtech/
http://www.zdnet.com/eweek/
http://macworld.zdnet.com/
http://www.macaddict.com/
http://www.google.com/
http://hotbot.lycos.com/
http://www.outpost.com
http://www.onvia.com
http://www.dictionary.com/
http://www.fatbrain.com/
http://www.smartpages.com/
http://www.zdnet.com/
http://bots.internet.com/

Cumulative Index

Supplement page numbers are preceded by "S"
and are printed in boldface: e.g., **S88-89**.